Using Rubrics to Monitor Outcomes in Occupational Therapy

Improve Critical Thinking and Clinical Reasoning by Adding Rubrics to Assess Goal Progress

Eleanor Cawley, M.S., OTR/L

Dedication

I dedicate this book

...to my son R.J. for all his encouragement during the process of writing this book. He constantly reminded me, 'You can do it mom. I am so proud of you.'

...to my mother, Eleanor, and my sister, Kathleen for all their support. Where would I be today, if were not for you yesterday?

...to Barbara Kornblau for reaching out, offering her expertise, her encouragement and good wishes as I started along my new adventure.

All of you have given me the courage to let out the writer inside and to take a chance.

Table of Contents

Table of Figures

About the Author

Eleanor Cawley is an occupational therapist with 15 years of experience in the pediatric sector, much of that time as an independent contractor. She is very passionate about her work and her writing. Ms. Eleanor, as she has been known by her students, has a Bachelor's of Science in Health Sciences and a Master's of Science in Occupational Therapy from Touro College. Since graduating as a non-traditional student, she has worked in a variety of settings throughout the life span but settled in the area of school-based therapy. She has a very keen interest in using technology to support independence and trains students to use programming not only to monitor their own goal progress but also support educational, vocational and life skills.

Another area of particular interest is documentation. As an independent contractor for many years, she feels that it is important to align methods of documenting goal progress with educators for greater consistency and understanding when writing for an IEP. Ms. Cawley feels that it is better to plan a format for documentation used in the IEP, such as for assessment and goal progress and that a rubric, in many ways, fulfills the need for consistency in documentation across all domains.

Combining her interest in technology and documentation, Ms. Cawley now uses Microsoft OneNote to maintain all documentation. She creates a digital notebook for each student or patient with any forms required uploaded as templates which can then be completed, and saved automatically.

Ms. Cawley strongly believes in student centered therapy. Students must be active participants in developing goals and documenting progress. In order to help students understand their progress, she teachers her students to develop electronic portfolios and to use spreadsheet programming with graphs to collect data and view progress, whenever possible.

Preface

After having my own struggles as a contract therapist in a public school setting, I decided to write this book to help me become more organized and clear in reporting present levels of performance and goal progress. Many times, due to budgetary and contractual concerns, a contract therapist is not privy to the professional development that district staff receives. Often times, we struggle to catch up with what teachers and district therapists are doing and floundering in the process

In my opinion, every therapist should be organized and have templates prepared for data collection on the typical skills that we would be working on in a school setting. I am a big proponent of "use what you have!" Keeping your templates in a storage system (i.e., the cloud or a USB drive), you will be able to retrieve and adapt templates to each new student without reinventing the wheel each time. I really do think in analytical concepts, my colleagues have expressed exactly that on many occasions. My thinking process has always been getting from point A to point B along a straight, well-defined line with the least amount of effort. Call it energy conservation, if you will, but thinking ahead, being efficient and having the answer at my fingertips without having to search, is a stress reliever. To that end, I have learned to use databases and templates to organize my report writing and data collection. In addition, to maintaining a consistent pattern of organization, I have developed a system of templates using Microsoft OneNote creating a digital notebook (folder) of notes, consults, initial evaluations and annual review forms. This ensures a complete and thorough documentation from initiation to discharge.

As you can see, I like making things easier for myself. The incorporation of checklists, forms and predefined goal progress notes, through the use of rubrics, ensures completeness not otherwise achieved. If I can take some time at the beginning of the school year, when I am refreshed and rejuvenated after having the summer off, to complete rubrics on my student's goals, I am a happy girl.

> "In the middle of difficulty lies opportunity."
>
> ~Albert Einstein

When given the opportunity, I like to align my methods of documentation with a teacher's for consistency and clarity. Unfortunately, not every teacher will meet or work with you and as a contract therapist, you may miss payment for your time. When methods of documentation do not align, it may cause confusion when writing reports for the annual review. Most often, rather than having a brief discussion, you are expected to "just do it." District employed support staff may be running your goals and not obtaining the same results since there is no explanation of how this goal is achieved. The methods used to assess goal progress contained in this book, clarifies what the occupational therapist is doing, and the step-wise method used to collect data toward goal progress with possible recommendations for the following school year. In my mind, if a teacher is using a rubric to determine a student's progress, for matters of consistency, all staff, monitoring that student's progress, should be using the same method of progress markers. To me, it only makes sense to standardize the methods of determining progress, recording daily documentation and then every IEP team member, including the parent and the student, will clearly understand how progress is determined and the direction any future intervention, if any, will take.

Introduction

A rubric is not meant to be a treatment plan but a method of marking goal progress. Treatment plans should be based on traditional occupational therapy framework models and the modalities that the therapist feels are appropriate. There are several ways to develop a rubric to assess treatment goals. One method may be to identify criteria and descriptors that indicate levels of assistance: 1. Hand over hand; 2. Compensatory strategies; 3. Additional time or prompts to complete the task and finally; 4. Independence. Another method might include using the motoric aspects: 1. Reach; 2. Grasp; 3. Release; and 4. Functional manipulation. Descriptors might include a percentage of task completed [25%, 50%, 75% and finally 100%] or a successful number of trials. Whatever method that you choose to use, make sure that your descriptors are concise, clearly measurable and easily understood for all those involved in using this rubric to assess this child's progress.

Training for staff may help with understanding the rubric and consistency between raters (evaluators). District staff using the rubric to assess a student's progress might include aides, teaching assistants, typically developing peers as mentors, teachers, substitute teachers, substitute aides, student teachers and sometimes, even parents. A variety of educational backgrounds, job training and life experiences contribute to the skills involved in using and understanding this rubric. So avoid jargon. For example, the word proprioception or proprioceptive unless, of course, you have provided an in-service to those involved, including a glossary of terms and have checked for understanding. Offer assistance whenever possible, don't make the school staff do research to understand what you have written. Chances are that most staff will not or even want to take the time to look up terms and concepts.

Chapter One

Good research requires planning, thought and open mindedness.

Accountability

Accountability is considered your obligation. "The obligation of an individual or organization to account for its activities, accept responsibility for them, and to disclose the results in a transparent manner." (Web Finance, Inc., 2013) Using the Occupational Therapy Practice Framework (AOTA, 2002) as a guide, interventions that address barriers to learning need to be based on three factors: 1. Evidence-based practice (EBP)/Effective Practice or "promising practice" (Swinth, Spencer, & Jackson, 2007); 2. Consistent results across all evaluators; and 3. Student Engagement. According to Dr. David Sackett (1996), EBP integrates clinical experience and expertise, patient values, and the best research evidence in the clinical decision making process. These factors offer the best opportunity for optimal outcomes and ultimately quality of life. According to Swinth et al (2007), "Given the state of the

> ### *Accountability*
>
> *Your obligation to account for your activities with a client and how a client responded to your treatment*

literature, providing effective (versus evidence-based) OT services may be the only realistic option when Level I and II studies are not available to guide intervention decisions. Interventions based on a careful reading of Level III, IV, or V studies combined with the systematic collection of individual student performance and outcome data can allow students to achieve targeted outcomes." In addition, when addressing educational outcomes, a student's progress needs to be seen as consistent by everyone that evaluates him or her. This can include teachers, aides or even peer mentors whose work with the student incorporates the student's goals. Lastly and most importantly, students must be aware of what their goals are; how they are being measured, expectations for achievement and how those goals [skills] will serve them throughout the rest of their life.

According to Swinth et al (2007), "The occupational therapist must develop a systematic way to document the OT intervention plan, its implementation, and student performance data." Additionally, Occupational therapists need to begin to think like researchers, and answer the following questions:

- What is the impact of the OT Intervention on the student's performance of educational activities?

- To what extent was the student's participation within the education context affected by the OT intervention?

Based on these factors, rubrics appear to be an effective method of marking progress, determining the efficacy of OT intervention and sustaining accountability which is then included in the Annual Review process.

Why Should Occupational Therapists Use Rubrics?

Ilene Ilott (2004) stated that she liked the term *research emergent* profession, "it epitomizes current stage of research and the aspirations for the future." She goes on to say that "Research emergent means that a profession lacks a solid tradition of research and thus infrastructure...to provide the evidence for evidence-based practice." This, she says, is because the research questions have neither been asked nor answered sufficiently. Thus the demand for research is due to the evidence-based movement and the cost constraints on the health care system.

When using a rubric to make judgments regarding a student's performance, we are using critical thinking skills to develop a standardized scoring method to assess progress and modify a rubric to fit the needs of the student. We are stating, exactly, our expectations of a student's progress

Why Should OTs Develop and Assess Progress Using Rubrics?

Occupational therapists need to think like researchers and scientists using systematic methods of data collection to determine the impact of our treatment methods on a student's performance in educational activities and the extent of a student's participation within the educational context affected by the OT intervention and a systematic method of modification of goals and treatment activities to gain the outcomes desired. This level of critical thinking, clinical reasoning, documentation and modification allows us to ask and answer questions pertaining to effective practice leading toward theories, hypotheses and eventually research studies.

Critical Thinking, Clinical Reasoning and Clinical Judgment

Critical thinking is a broad term used to define the complex process that requires focus to get the results you need in various situations, both inside and outside of a clinical setting. It means not accepting information at face value without evaluating it for good fit for your patient, your student. *Critical thinking* is a skill that flows and changes based on the demands of the situation. Your knowledge, skills, experience and hands on practice determine your proficiency in critical thinking.

Clinical reasoning is a more specific term referring to ways that you think about patient care [determination, management and prevention] and problems. *Clinical judgment* is the outcome of critical thinking and clinical reasoning. (Alfaro-LeFevre, 2013)

According to Rogers (1983), therapists from many settings use clinical reasoning skills to collect and transform data about patients into decisions that have critical implications for the patient's quality of life. She states, "The possibility of error in our clinical judgments and the potential ensuing negative consequences urge us to develop ways of improving our assessment and treatment decisions." This correlates with Bateman and Herr (2010), in that we have an ethical and legal responsibility to structure our goals and progress markers to be clear, concise and relevant so that we gain the maximum amount of information about how and how much the student learns.

Much of the occupational therapy literature regarding clinical reasoning revolves around the work of Joan C. Rogers and her Eleanor Clark Slagle Lecture (1983). Rogers reported her findings from a study she conducted on a small number of occupational therapists. She stated, 'My research…, suggests that our cognitive processes are regarded as intuitive and ineffable." Cognitive activity is the heart, the core of clinical enterprise and failure to understand the process of that which underlies our practice, precludes an adequate description of clinical reasoning. She goes on to state, "This in turn prevents the development of a methodology for systematically improving it and for teaching it."

Thinking like a Researcher

The entire educational system, from preschool through college, is changing with schools scrambling to develop computational and critical thinking programs and engaging students in "thinking like a scientist." Occupational therapists also need to think like scientists [researchers] in the way that they plan treatment strategies and systematically collect data to evaluate the efficacy of our work with students, patients and clients.

As a research emergent profession, it is incumbent upon us to find ways to demonstrate and justify what we do and how we do it. For the purposes of transparency in accountability, a rubric allows us to anticipate student outcomes [using descriptors] and structure our documentation to systematically collect and subsequently analyze our data efficiently.

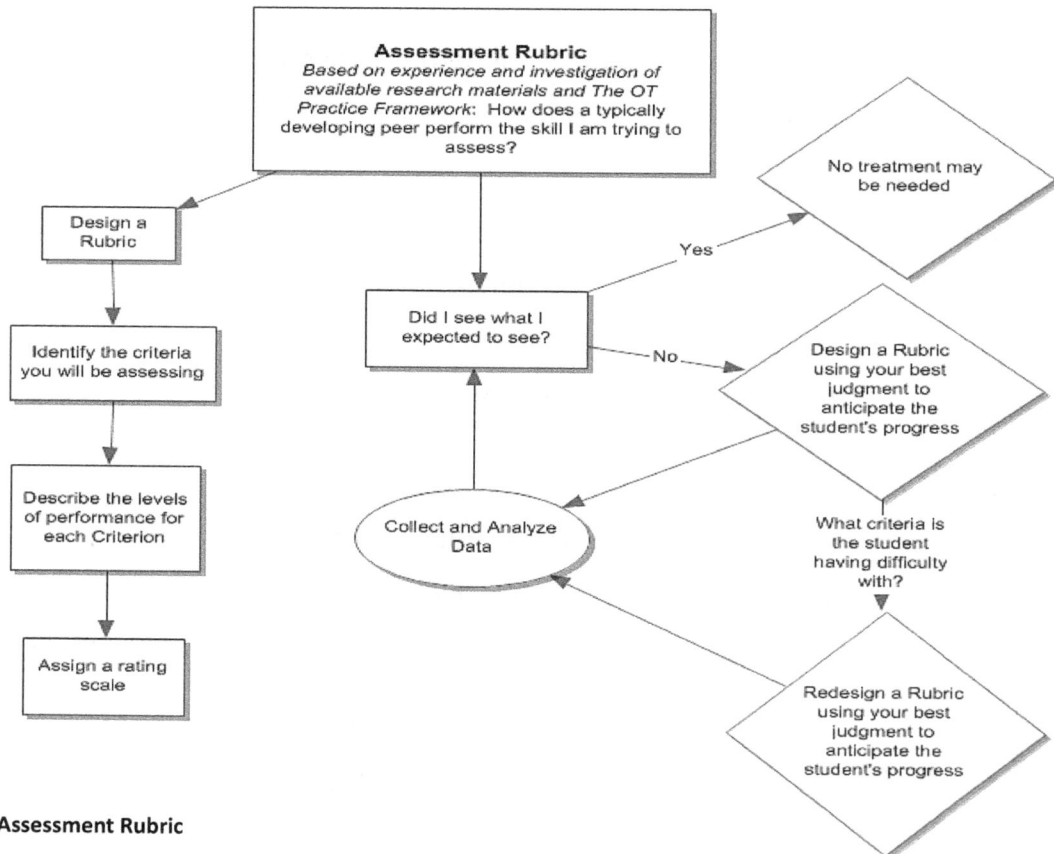

Figure 1: Assessment Rubric

Chapter Two

"The more transparent the learning objectives and expectations, the greater the likelihood that learners will achieve them." (Ehrmann, Unknown)

What is a Rubric?

Various dictionaries define a rubric as a set of *rules*. In this case, *rules* that are used to make a judgment regarding a student's level of performance. Rubrics identify the standard of performance. It is a way of communicating what is expected, describing a level of performance and the associated quality. Rubrics are considered to be an *authentic assessment*. An *authentic assessment* uses real-life criteria to evaluate a students' work [product] (Pearson Education, Inc. , 2000-2013). A student centered approach, or rubric, can help a student understand and make judgments about his or her own work. According to Heidi Andrade (Andrade, 2000-2008), students should be able to use rubrics in the same way as teachers do: clarifying the standards for a quality of performance, and guide ongoing feedback towards the standards. According to many teachers using rubrics (Zelkowitz, 2009), "It is far easier for students to grasp benchmark objectives to perform at each level of mastery using a well-written rubric."

Common features of scoring rubrics (Contributors, 2012) include:

1. Focus on measuring a stated objective (performance, behavior, or quality)

2. Uses a range [rating scale] to judge performance

3. Contains specific performance characteristics (criteria/descriptors) to indicate which and when a standard has been met

Based on an article from Wikipedia (Contributors, 2012) a rubric is a set of standardized developmental ratings to support self-reflection and self-assessment, delineates consistent criteria for grading and provides communication between the assessor and those being assessed. "In this new

> ### *Rubric*
>
> *Rules; Judgments*
>
> *Communicating what is expected.*
>
> *Authentic Assessment*

sense, a scoring rubric is a set of criteria and standards typically linked to learning objectives. It is used to assess or communicate about product, performance, or process tasks." Once the rubric is completed, it provides a direction for subsequent learning or teaching.

Typically, rubrics specify the performance expected for several levels of quality. These levels of quality may be ratings (e.g., Excellent, Good, Needs Improvement) or numerical scores (e.g., 4, 3, 2, 1) which are then utilized to determine an alphanumeric grade (e.g., A, B, C, etc). Rubrics provide an objective and consistent way to assess subjective tasks, indicate what is expected, and highlight how performance will be evaluated. Determining if a scoring rubric is an appropriate evaluation technique depends upon the purpose of the assessment.

Advantages and Disadvantages of Using Rubrics for an Assessment

While it can be time consuming to develop a rubric, an effective rubric allows for great objectivity and consistency (Dodge, 2007). Creating a rubric forces the therapist to define and clarify criteria in specific terms. It allows the student, the therapist and anyone else who is evaluating the student to understand exactly what is expected and how the therapist will determine if the goal or objective has been achieved. Each criterion then becomes a benchmark by which to assess and document a student's progress. According to Wolf and Stevens (2007), a student who is unable to understand a curriculum that is "hidden," cannot be expected to guess what the expectations are and will be more at risk than those students who "know how to play the game." According to Zelkowitz (2009), "Another benefit to using rubrics is that they are easily interpreted by a variety of school staff members as well as parents, and thus enable them to be more included in the IEP process." In the case of the rubrics found in this publication, any report generated from the data that you collect will also give the parent a clear assessment of their child's status on any OT related skill assessed.

According to Carnegie Mellon (2012), a carefully designed rubric offers additional benefits for both the teacher [therapist] and the student. In terms of occupational therapy services, using a rubric to assess goal progress allows the therapist to: 1. Reduce time spent writing long progress notes that lack clarity. 2. Clearly identify strengths and weaknesses in attaining progress. 3. Ensure consistency across time and raters. 4. Reduce uncertainty that often accompanies assessing levels of progress. 5. Reduces student complaints about progress reports. In this case, particularly for an older student, clarity of the goal, its purpose and how achievement is determined, decreases that level of anxiety of having to be in OT while in middle and high school. 6. Students are better able to understand the therapist's expectations. 7. Better use of therapist feedback. 8. Students can better recognize their own strengths and weaknesses while being able to redirect their efforts with increased independence.

Tips for Rubric Development

The rubrics contained in this publication are not the only opportunity for an occupational therapist to use a rubric with their students. There are many other goals that an occupational therapist may develop that can be assessed by a rubric. Clearly, a student may require strategies to meet the criteria set forth in this rubric. For example, when handwriting, a student may not be grasping the pencil appropriately and will require a rubric that assesses his or her progress from "delayed" or "impaired" to "typical" or "no impairment."

Collaboration with teachers and staff will provide additional opportunities for rubric development and assessments of a student's performance within the classroom and being able to incorporate occupational therapy strategies to meet the needs of each classroom activity. When developing a rubric, incorporate the following:

- ✓ Use specific descriptors to meet the criteria that identify acceptable performance at each scoring level
- ✓ Criteria and descriptors should be clear [free of jargon], concise and in a step-wise progression
- ✓ Make sure that your criteria does not overlap and that there is no more than 5 criteria on which to make a judgment
- ✓ Rubrics should have 3-5 performance levels with assigned scores or descriptive terms
- ✓ Use short, simple statements directly related to anticipated outcomes
- ✓ Each level in the rubric should focus on a different aspect of the skill [i.e., reach, grasp, release, functional manipulation].
- ✓ Criterion for each step should be measurable

- ✓ Students must be fully aware of what they are expected to do
- ✓ Keep individual skill rubrics to a minimum to fit on a single sheet of paper
- ✓ Review and reevaluate your rubric to make sure that the criteria are understandable for all staff assessing the student through the rubric. Avoid vague terms like "know," "organized manner," "correctly," "seems," "little," "mostly," "adequate," "some," "weak," and "neatly." Clarify what you mean.
    - o **S-P-E-L-L-I-T-O-U-T**
- ✓ Just as students need to be aware of what is expected, so should any other staff members using the rubric. Use clear, concise descriptions in each performance level and avoid any opportunity for a subjective judgment
- ✓ When designing your rubric, make sure that there is space for comments, adding additional space on the back for more comments
- ✓ Limit the number of criteria in your rubric. Assess components of a task until mastered then redefine your rubric to assess the entire task

The rubrics, contained within this publication, consider tasks that are typical skills required for school related activities. If tasks have not been mastered then you have an opportunity to develop your own rubric to assess each component based on the individual needs of the student. It does not provide treatment protocols or modalities, as the treatment plan varies with each individual student and is based on need, underlying factors, a therapist background, training and experiences.

How Do Rubrics Relate to the IEP?

According to Zelkowitz (2009), some might consider that a rubric developed by a teacher or therapist is not a universal assessment with results varying upon the person who interprets them. She goes on to say that rubrics are a better method to determine progress markers, since they are designed to "meet the particular goals and short-term objectives of each student."

According to Bateman, et al (2010), the IDEA no longer requires that an IEP include short-term objectives and benchmarks. They are urging that IEP teams continue to use short-term objectives and benchmarks for "compelling educational and legal reasons." Some consider it courting educational, legal and financial disaster to report progress without measurable and measured progress markers. Once the IEP is developed with measurable annual goals, strategies should be developed with either short-term objectives or benchmarks that will lead to completion of the overall goal. You will have to consider the needs of the IEP team, which includes parents and students, to monitor goal progress and revise the IEP, as warranted, consistent with the student's needs and abilities. It should be noted that benchmarks are required only for those students who are assessed under No Child Left Behind, using an alternate method of assessment other than grade level standards. This includes goals developed by related service providers.

Benchmarks for any student can clarify how achievement of the goal will be judged and the steps needed to achieve that goal. What is very important to consider when writing a goal is "Is it measurable?" What are you measuring? How are you measuring it? In their book, *Writing Measurable IEP Goals and Objectives*, (Bateman & Herr, 2010) state that the goal reveals what to measure, yields the same conclusion if measured by several people, allows a calculation of how much progress has been made and can be measured without any additional information.

So let's take a look at a goal, add benchmarks and see how this works. This is a goal for a young boy named George. A new staff member, therapist or teacher, without knowing anything about this child, can at least understand what is expected of him to complete this goal. The goal states, "When provided with Benbow scissors, George will be able to grasp the scissors in a thumb's up position with the preferred hand to cut simple shapes [circle, square, and triangle], rotating the shapes as he cuts, within 1/8th inch of the boundary line in 8/10 trials over 4 weeks." This goal measures George's ability to cut shapes within a specific degree of accuracy with a particular type of scissors. He is expected to achieve that level of performance on 8 out of 10 occasions. Since prompts are not listed in the goal or description, George should be able to achieve this goal and be independent when using scissors, as described. Please note that Benbow Scissors are considered "learning scissors" and can be purchased for either a right or left handed student. It would be very important for the therapist to have already identified the handedness of this student so that he is presented with the correct pair of scissors.

Under the goal listed in the table, there are columns labeled 1 through 4. The numbers represent the scores attained each time George completes that portion of the task, the benchmark. The columns, labeled 1 through 4, can represent only the score for the level of achievement but can also represent the level of achievement anticipated in each marking period or in this case each quarter. Comments, the last column, can include the following: 1. the number and type of prompts needed; 2. any difficulties that the student might have had; 3. any spontaneous modifications that were made (i.e., scissors were handed to the student in the correct position and not placed on the table); 4. the media that the student was able to cut (i.e., Theraputty, Playdoh, straws, cardstock, etc.). If, at the end of the first 4 weeks, George is not meeting the criteria, the goal/benchmark might need to be reassessed and modified to meet his needs. For example, if George is not placing his fingers into the scissors loops when placed on the table top but will place his fingers into the loops when the scissors are oriented vertically and handed to him, the 1st benchmark or criteria may need to be changed to include prompts or to hand him the scissors. You might consider using a data collection sheet for each goal George might have. If you notice, there are check boxes in columns 3 and 4. For clarity in reporting progress, a new sheet should be provided each time a task is completed. For example, let's say that George is able to cut on a line. Once he has achieved that benchmark, a new data collection sheet should be provided for cutting out a square and then again for cutting out a triangle.

In the following individual skill rubric, the data collection is set-up for 10 weeks. Ten weeks is the typical length of a quarter in a 40 week school year. When data is collected, make sure that the data corresponds to the correct week in the school year. So, if a new sheet is generated during week 8, the new data collection sheet should contain data for weeks 8, 9 and 10. As you can see, the rubric and accompanying data is included on one sheet of paper with space for additional comments on the reverse side. Using this method of data collection and progress markers makes progress reporting simple and concise. Your quarterly progress reports, with data collected by multiple evaluators, will go quickly and without question. Another benefit of using rubrics, once you have your rubrics made and save them on your computer from year to year, you only need to change a few items to personalize the rubric to transfer it from one student to another. So as you can see, the educational placement may not impact on benchmarks for George, at all. What is clear is that no matter what a student's placement, clearly written criteria and descriptors to assess progress [benchmarks] helps the IEP Team come together for the benefit of the student.

Types of Rubrics

"A *holistic rubric* consists of a single scale with all criteria to be included in the evaluation being considered together (e.g., clarity, organization, and mechanics). With a holistic rubric the rater assigns a single score (usually on a 1 to 4 or 1 to 6 point scale) based on an overall judgment of the student's work. The rater matches an entire piece of student work to a single description on the scale" (De Paul University, 2001-2012).

"An *analytic rubric* resembles a grid with the criteria for a student product listed in the leftmost column and with levels of performance listed across the top row often using numbers and/or descriptive tags. The cells within the center of the rubric may be left blank or may contain descriptions of what the specified criteria look like for each level of performance. When scoring with an analytic rubric each of the criteria is scored individually" (De Paul University, 2001-2012)

In the opinion of this writer, an analytic rubric is more in line with task analysis and fits the needs of progress in occupational therapy.

Rubrics

Holistic		Analytic	
• Single Scale • Single Score • Single Descriptor		• Multiple Scales • Multiple Scores • Multiple Descriptors	
Advantages	**Disadvantages**	**Advantages**	**Disadvantages**
Shows what the student is able to do. Rater needs to make fewer decisions Rater training improves reliability.	Does not show what the student cannot do Inconsistent performance over the span of criteria points, make it difficult to select the single best score Criteria cannot be weighted.	Demonstrates areas of strength and weakness. Criterion can be weighted to reflect the relative importance of each dimension.	Time consuming to create and use due to number of traits assessed Useless unless descriptors are clear, concise and understood by all raters so that they can arrive at the same score

Table 1: Types of Rubrics

Goal: When provided with Benbow scissors, using his preferred hand, George will be able to grasp the scissors in a thumb's up position to cut simple shapes [circle, square, and triangle], rotating the shapes as he cuts, within $1/8^{th}$ inch of the boundary line on 8 out of 10 occasions over 4 weeks. [Within □ ½ inch □ ¼ inch □ 1/8 inch of the boundary line]

1 Reach	2 Grasp	3 Release	4 Functional Manipulation	Comments
When the scissors are placed on a table top in front of George with handles pointed toward him near his midline, he will place his thumb and middle fingers into the scissors loops with index finger placed outside and in front of the lower loop on 8 out of 10 occasions. [*Midline indicates the center of the body*]	Once George has met the criteria for #1 [Reach], he will then rotate his forearm, bringing the scissors to a thumb's up position. With his non-dominant hand he will then insert the paper or other media into the scissors on 8 out of 10 occasions. [*4th and 5th fingers of the preferred hand should be curled toward the palm of his hand*]	Once George has met the criteria for #1 [Reach] and #2 [Grasp] he will : □ Snip the paper in 8/10 trials **OR** □ Make sequential cuts along the boundaries of the line/shape on 8 out of 10 occasions. [*4th and 5th fingers of the preferred hand should remain stationary*]	Once George has met the for #1 [Reach], #2 [Grasp] and #3 [Release] he will: □ Cut on a line on 8 out of 10 occasions **OR** □ Cut out a square rotating at the corners on 8 out of 10 occasions **OR** □ Cut out a triangle rotating at the corners on 8 out of 10 occasions **OR** □ Cut out a circle rotating as he cuts in on 8 out of 10 occasions	

Additional Information: Benbow scissors are very sharp and should be used under supervision only. A score of zero is entered when George did not meet Criteria 1 in any trial. Trials indicate the number of correct trials out of 10. Trials are conducted in sets of 10 only. For example, George might score 1 in 4/10 trials in one day.

1st Quarter	Monday		Tuesday		Wednesday		Thursday		Friday	
	Score	# of Trials	Score	# of Trials	Score	# of Trials	Score	# of Trials	Score	# of Trials
Week 1 Date:										
Week 2 Date:										
Week 3 Date:										
Week 4 Date:										
Week 5 Date:										
Week 6 Date:										
Week 7 Date:										
Week 8 Date:										
Week 9 Date:										
Week 10 Date:										

Table 2: This is an example of a Individual skill rubric with benchmarks for a cutting with scissors goal.

Just a Word on Organization

When working in a school, it is easy for paperwork and tools to be misplaced. A binder with a ringed pencil case attached and page protectors for your originals, is most effective. The pencil case is attached to the binder by the rings and contains the items that the therapist is recommending [pencil grip, scissors, spacing guide, etc.]. Page protectors should contain clean and clear copies of the rubric and other supporting materials like a student checklist, exercise booklet, copy of exercise video or staff training. Also recommended is a log in sheet so that you can identify the staff person who worked with a student on any particular day. This can determine if the student's success or lack of is attributed to staff interactions with the student.

Staff Log-In Sheet			
Date	Time Start/End	Signature	Initials

Table 3: Sample of Staff Log-In Sheet

Chapter Three

A balanced system of assessments measures the skill

at the end of treatment and improves learning during treatment

Occupational Therapy Assessment

Rogers (1983) explored clinical questions regarding an occupational therapy assessment. She considered the assessment to be a concise and accurate summary of the patient's role performance. This is particularly important in a school-based assessment. A school-based assessment includes a reason for the referral [the problems that the student is having in the classroom], and his or her motivation for educational activities. In my opinion, motivation can be broken down in to at least two components: skill and desire. If a student has limited or no skill in a particular area, there will be no desire to engage in the activity.

The Importance of a Detailed Referral

Identifies the problems that the student is having

Less time wasted in searching for problems where none exist

Improved selection of assessment methods

Improved selection of interview questions

Improved recommendations upon completion of the assessment

Based on the referral, an occupational therapist designs a plan for evaluation. Without a detailed referral, much time and energy is wasted on weeding out any potential problems. In almost all OT evaluations in a public school setting, a therapist would conduct one or two standardized assessments [i.e., visual perceptual and visual motor], a handwriting assessment, and a keyboarding assessment. In addition, we would interview the student and hopefully the teacher(s). Hopefully all of this will reveal the reason the student was recommended for an occupational therapy evaluation. Sometimes it doesn't. Very often the student did not even know that he or she was recommended for evaluation. Even though an appointment was scheduled days in advance, everyone has been notified and the parent has signed consent, someone has neglected to tell the student. This is definitely an issue for compliance on the part of the student. If you are a contractor and new to the building, staff may be hesitant to provide information as they are not sure about consent to speak with you. So as you can see, the roadblocks to understanding the true nature of a student's problems are many.

A student's strengths should be highlighted and built upon. Not only should an occupational therapy assessment explore problem areas but also what the student can do and how well they do it.

The use of a rubric in an occupational therapy evaluation can answer a number of questions that a standardized test cannot. Rogers (1983) said so eloquently, "This is what I expect to find, now what do I find?" When using a rubric for assessing skills, the criteria identify what I would expect to see in a typically developing peer. For example: Assessing a 10 year old female for handwriting skills, I would expect to see a dynamic tripod grasp, good letter formation for all 26 letters of the alphabet, good spacing between letters and word, and good line regard. How different is this student from the typically developing peer? If you have developed a rubric to assess handwriting skills, you will be able to explain how different this student actually is. What did you find?

A detailed referral can limit the parameters of the assessment. We don't need to conduct a SIPT when visual perceptual testing will suffice. We need to know how much data should be collected and when to stop based on "ethical consequences of an error in judgment." (Rogers, 1983) The randomness that comes from the lack of a good referral can lead to a student not getting therapy or getting therapy when a consult with good recommendations would suffice. A detailed referral can be nothing more than "the student is having problems with handwriting" with a handwriting sample obtained from the student's notebook. That spontaneous sample is another example of portfolio materials that can be added to create a balanced assessment. We are then looking at standardized and non-standardized assessments as well as a collection of interviews and structured clinical observations and skill assessments using rubrics.

A Balance between Standardized and Non-Standardized Assessments

Whether you are determining progress for annual review or evaluating for the first time occupational therapists need to conduct a variety of assessments, including an interview of the student and clinical observations. During the time for annual review[1], therapists and teachers are asked to provide an update on the student's goal progress and to give input as to what the student might need for the coming school year. In some locales therapists are asked to conduct standardized assessments[2] yearly while others require testing every three years. Whether standardized testing is administered or not also depends on the educational placement of the student [i.e., alternate assessment]. Whatever regulations a district has to follow, a therapist is asked to provide detailed and accurate reporting of a student's Present Levels of Performance [PLOPS] and progress toward completing his or her goals every year.

There are a number of methods of documenting a student's performance level and progress. Of course, the first method is standardized testing. This type of testing generates a score and compares one student's performance on a particular test to that of other examinees; other students of the same age group who have taken this assessment. Examples of standardized testing used in school-based occupational therapy include the Developmental Test of Visual Perception-2 (DTVP-2) and the Bruininks-Oseretsky Test of Motor Proficiency, Second Edition (BOT-2). Another type of testing is called a criterion-referenced assessment. A criterion-referenced assessment is when a student's "performance is compared to a pre-defined set of criteria or a standard" (Reier, 2008). According to Ms. Reier (2008), the goal of this type of assessment is to determine whether or not a student can demonstrate mastery of a skill or a skill set. Examples of criterion-referenced testing used in school-based occupational therapy

---

[1] At least once a year, a child's IEP team (parents, child, classroom and special education teachers, school administrators and specialists) are required to gather to review and evaluate the effectiveness of the child's current IEP document, establish goals for the coming year and revise the IEP as needed to reflect the results of recent evaluations, changes in needs, etc. to make sure the plan maximizes the child's skills and abilities. (The Minnesota Governor's Council on Developmental Disabilities, 2011)

[2] A Standardized test is a test that is given in a consistent or "standard" manner. Standardized tests are designed to questions, administration procedures, and scoring procedures. When a standardized test is administered, is it done so according to certain rules and specifications so that testing conditions are the same for all test takers (The Johnson Center, 2013)

settings are the *Sensorimotor Performance Analysis* (SPA) and *The Print Tool Evaluation* from Handwriting without Tears.

> *Standardized testing is considered a "snapshot" of a student's performance on a particular day, at a particular time.*

Another way of assessing a student's performance level is through a portfolio of a student's work over the school year. According to (Glor-Scheib, 2007), there are three basic types of portfolios: 1. Documentation; 2. Process; 3. Showcase. Another way of documenting a student's progress is through task analysis, checklists and rubrics. These methods align more closely with what an occupational therapist is used to in terms of clinical observation. Using structured methods of observation and clinical documentation improve the qualitative and quantitative aspects of documentation. Task analysis is "a step by step direction list of how to complete either a physical or mental task" (Hembree, 2010). Once a task analysis is developed and refined, it becomes the basis from which we, as therapists, structure our observations. The rubric, based on criteria developed through task analysis, provides us with the structure to score a student, with consistency, across evaluators.

A More Complete Picture

Conducting standardized testing is not enough to gain an accurate picture of how a student is functioning in the classroom. While testing might provide an indicator for deficits, it certainly does not provide the video of a student's function over time. Standardized testing is considered a "snapshot" of a student's performance on a particular day, at a particular time. A number of other methods need to be used to gain an accurate assessment of the student's abilities.

Interview

An interview may be one of the most important components of an assessment. A structured interview format, such as The Student Interview (Cawley, 2011) or The School Setting Interview (Hemmingsson, Egilson, Hoffman, & Keilhofner, 2005) can provide valuable information that the student may not reveal through other means. Sometimes when a student is provided with multiple formats, such as verbal and written methods to contribute to an evaluation, much more is revealed than through standard verbal interview. The student is prompted to answer questions through checklist and paragraph formats. Once the student completes the written components, the interview can be reviewed with the student for further details and can be confirmed with the parent and/or teacher.

Clinical Observations

Your observations are extremely important when evaluating a student for an initial or triennial evaluation and annual review. As previously indicated, standardized testing is only a snapshot of what the student is capable of on the day the testing was administered. At this point, it would be prudent to consider the student's status on this day. If the student is ill, has had other testing or is not cooperative for some reason, it may not be the best day for you to test this student. Another day may provide more accurate testing, and should be considered, if at all possible. Get to know your administrators and their preferences.

It is a good idea to provide structure to your observations. For example, there are skills that you may need to report on, such as keyboarding, for which there is currently no formalized testing. A rubric provides a structure to your clinical judgments when assessing the student's keyboarding skills that may be consistent across evaluators. Many teachers may conduct a keyboarding assessment as well and may even be using the keyboarding rubric provided in this book. Since this is a rubric and not a standardized test, it is expected to be administered by more than one evaluator, giving more of a complete picture of the student's keyboarding abilities. Remember a rubric is meant to have consistent scores across evaluators. Any well-written rubric will work and can be administered by any evaluator.

The benefit of using any well-written rubric developed and administered by an occupational therapist is that the OT is trained in not only the cognitive, sensory and self-regulation components of a task but also the motor components and can give a better assessment of the motor skills and any possible impairments which may impact on the student's performance in any given task. An occupational therapist can provide additional in sight to why the student may not be achieving the desired outcomes.

Methods of Assessment

- Standardized Testing
  - Compares a student to other examinees
  - Generates a score
    - DTVP-A, DTVP2, VMI, TVPS, MVPT, Bender
- Non-standardized Testing
  - Criterion Referenced
    - Performance is compared to a pre-defined set of criteria or a standard
    - SFA, SMPA
  - Interviews
  - Portfolios
    - Documentation
    - Process
    - Showcase
  - Performance observations
    - Can also be a rubric

Types of Portfolios
[Student's Product]

- Documentation
  - Demonstrates growth toward a particular standard
    - Includes samples of student's work
- Process
  - Shows the phases of a student's learning
- Showcase
  - Shows accomplishments and mastery of learning standards; A tool for participation and communication that shows a student's abilities, interests, points of pride and perceived strengths [e-portfolios]

Performance
[Clinical Observations]

- Task Analysis
  - a step by step list of directions on how to complete a task
- Checklists
  - Usually a yes or no format
    - A visual picture or prompts
  - An observation or self-assessment tool
- Rubrics
  - a standard of performance
  - a way of communicating what is expected
  - describing performance levels and associated quality
  - rules for making a judgment on student performance
  - consistency across evaluators

Table 4: Methods of Assessment

Chapter Four

Good grief! Can I be expected to make a rubric for everything?

Components of a Rubric

> **Components of a Rubric**
>
> *A Goal or Standard*
>
> *Rating Scale*
>
> *Criteria*
>
> *Descriptors*
>
> *Comments*

The components of a rubric include: a. measurable goal/objective, benchmark or statement based on a standard on which you are trying to determine progress; b. a scoring system [performance level/rating scale]; c. the criteria that you are trying to assess; d. clear, concise descriptors; and a section for comments. Remember that the rubric is the measurement tool. The rubric contains the *rules* that define how you measure progress.

Goal/Objective/Benchmark

For an occupational therapist, this is what we expect the student to be able to do, by the end of the school year. How would you determine if a child has accomplished this goal and would another evaluator come to the same conclusion? The goal must be "measured as written without any referring to additional or external information" (Bateman & Herr, 2010) Much more about goals in Chapter Five.

Scoring/Rating Scales

This provides a numeric or descriptive assessment of the student's progress. Using words to describe a student's performance might be reinforcing to the student, particularly when you use terms meaningful to the student. Although the words poor, minimal, average and above average may be fine for your documentation, when discussing progress with a student it might be beneficial to use other words, such as game related terms or even slang appropriate to the student's age or situation. Using these terms may encourage the student to continue to participate.

Descriptive Terms to Rate Performance			
Descriptive Terms Can be Meaningful to the Student to Promote Engagement*			
1	**2**	**3**	**4**
• Beginning Skill	• Limited Skill	• Some Proficiency	• Proficient
• Novice	• Intermediate	• Advanced	• Expert
• Poor	• Minimal	• Average	• Above Average
• Emerging	• Developing	• Acceptable	• Accomplished
• Try Again	• Making Progress	• Almost There	• Master
• Newbie	• Evolving	• Intensifying	• Ultimate
• First Base	• Second Base	• Third Base	• Home Run!

Table 5: Descriptive Terms to Rate Student's Performance

Criteria

That part of the task, the *principle* that is being measured. The criteria determine how well the student is meeting the goal. For example: When assessing handwriting skills, one criterion that an occupational therapist might include is line regard. In other words, using well-written descriptors to make a judgment on line regard, is the student's handwriting sitting appropriately on the line, floating above or sinking below?

Descriptors

Descriptors are clear and concise explanations of the criteria or steps of the task that need to be met in order to assess progress. This is that part of the rubric that allows different evaluators to come to the same conclusion when assessing goal progress. It is the *rule* or the *test* that allows one to determine if the criteria has been met. For example: The student will write 10 letters on the line not above or below the line 8/10 times.

Comments

A key factor in any good rubric is clear comments relevant to the descriptor(s). For example: The descriptor states that the student will place his thumb and middle fingers into the scissors loops with index finger placed outside and in front of the lower loop. However, the student is not grasping the scissors in the way described. "George grasped the scissors with index and thumb" would be a good point to share with the therapist or other members of the team. If his grasping pattern continues, the rubric might need to be modified. Refrain from saying things like, "George had a bad day" or "George is refusing to hold the scissors correctly." While George may have had a rough day, or is not holding the scissors as described, it may be because of something that happen outside of OT activities or due to an impairment of hand function and may or may not be relevant to the rubric. If there are questions or concerns about the rubric, student performance, understanding the descriptors, etc., it may be better to attach a sticky note to the rubric or write the comments on a separate sheet of paper. That way, any comments written on the rubric itself remain directly related to the rubric.

Individual Skill Rubric

This is a system that I use occasionally to address simple sequential goals, such as cutting with scissors, which does not need any modifications and assumes that prerequisite skills, such as posture and hand strength are considered adequate for the task. In an individual skill rubric, we are looking at single descriptors to meet criteria. This may be used for short-term therapy [or assessment of a single skill] where only the most simplistic criterion [possibly just sequencing] needs to be met. A rubric in this format will allow efficient data collection to determine goal progress and mastery. If the student is not meeting the goal based on this simple style of rubric, then there may be another problem which can be explored through an analytic rubric. The beauty of a system of well-defined rubrics is that is allows us to locate problems, modify the task and the rubric to meet the needs of the student.

Analytic Rubric

An analytic rubric is a criterion referenced assessment with the criteria separated in to discrete tasks. This format can be used for initial assessment of skills and determine the amount of progress in more complex skill areas such as keyboarding, handwriting, shoe tying, dressing, etc. This type of rubric can be diagnostic if the appropriate criteria are being assessed. For example: You might include criterion, such as following verbal directions; identifying right and left on self, on others, in the environment; or responding to sound.

There are many instances when a therapist may not be present but goals will be worked on (run). Goals are typically run in an alternately assessed classroom, group home situations, day programs, etc. when the therapist is not present. When specific criteria are not outlined for staff to determine the student's response to the activity, it is very difficult to document the student's response to the intervention and have a consensus between raters. What we are left with is poor data collection and documentation and not necessarily the response of the student to the treatment or intervention. Detailing the anticipated outcome through the use of a well-written rubric provides a therapist the opportunity to assess the effect a treatment has on function.

A school-based therapist's treatment plan might call for an exercise plan to prepare the student for writing activities. Typically, a therapist might provide an exercise plan to the teacher and/or parent for carryover. We can develop a rubric for a specific exercise plan and another to assess the functional activity connected to the exercise plan. We would be looking for a number of outcomes: 1. Increased independence with the exercise plan. 2. Goal progress related to the functional activity [i.e., handwriting]. A sample rubric is contained in Table 5. Depending on the student and staff, you may need to be more specific, adding additional materials, such as a checklist for the student, staff training forms, or maybe a video of the staff training. You may have to include specific directives for the staff to use if you have modified a task for the student. If you provide a video of your exercise plan be generic so that it does not have to be made repeatedly. For example: based on the rubric in Table 5, make a video of upper extremity exercises that is searchable not the student's exercise plan. Factors that can have an effect on the accuracy of data collection for a rubric include:

- Cultural beliefs and primary language of the staff person.
- Educational background
- Level of training for their position
- Reading level/ability to understand the rubric for both staff and student
- Amount of training and support that you provide
- Your ability to set-up/organize documents and materials
- Staff interaction with the student
- The environment

Student's Name:		Date Initiated:
		Date Ended:

GOAL	When provided with picture prompts and checklists, the student will be independent in performing an exercise program to support fine motor skills program, from set-up to clean-up, in 1/2 trials on 5 consecutive occasions.					
	CRITERIA	1	2	3	4	
SET-UP	Gathered Supplies	Student will use picture prompts to gather the prescribed supplies with 3 verbal prompts	Student will use picture prompts to gather the prescribed supplies with 2 verbal prompts	Student will use picture prompts to gather the prescribed supplies with 1 verbal prompt	Student will use picture prompts to gather the prescribed supplies without verbal prompts	
	Wash Hands	Using picture prompts, student will turn on water and wet hands	Using picture prompts, student will pump soap into hands from dispenser 2x	Using picture prompts. student will rub all surfaces of both hands with lather for 20 seconds	Using picture prompts, student will rinse hands, get paper towel, dry hands and turn off water using paper towel	
EXERCISE PROGRAM	Using Theraputty	Student will open and invert container, squeeze the bottom to release theraputty	On the table top, student will roll theraputty into a snake with open hands 2x	On the table top, student will roll the theraputty into a ball with open hands, flatten the ball and spread it out using his fingertips 2x	Student will roll the theraputty into a ball with open hands, place it into the container and close the lid.	
	Bilateral Upper Extremity Exercises with #1 weights	Student will perform shoulder flexion/extension exercises with visual model x10 reps	Student will perform shoulder abduction with visual model x 10 reps	Student will perform Bicep curls with visual model x10 reps	Student will perform wrist flexion & Extension with visual model x10 reps	
CLEAN UP	Replace Supplies	Using picture prompts, student will return supplies [weights and theraputty] to storage location with 3 verbal prompts	Using picture prompts, student will return supplies [weights and theraputty] to storage location with 2 verbal prompts	Using picture prompts, student will return supplies [weights and theraputty] to storage location with 1 verbal prompts	Using picture prompts, student will return supplies [weights and theraputty] to storage location without verbal prompts	

Data Collection   **Week of:**

	Monday		Tuesday		Wednesday		Thursday		Friday	
Set Up	Score	Trials	Score	Trials	Score	Trials	Score	Trials	Score	Trials
Gather Supplies										
Wash Hands										
Exercise Program	Score	Trials	Score	Trials	Score	Trials	Score	Trials	Score	Trials
Theraputty										
Weights										
Clean-Up	Score	Trials	Score	Trials	Score	Trials	Score	Trials	Score	Trials
Replace Supplies										

Date:	Comments:

Table 5: Sample Analytic Rubric with data collection

Holistic Rubric

A holistic rubric provides a score for the entire task. When assessing a skill using a holistic rubric in occupational therapy, a narrative is beneficial to explain what is seen and is probably not the best type of rubric to use for motor tasks. You might find that a holistic rubric is just the thing when assessing handwriting a paragraph.

Name:		Date:
Score	Criteria	
4	• Student completed 3 sentences • With line regard • Without erasures • In the time allotted	
3	• Student completed 3 sentences • With line regard • Without erasures	
2	• Student completed 3 sentences • With line regard.	
1	• Student completed 3 sentences.	

Table 6: Sample Holistic Rubric

Although a holistic rubric may be effective in some circumstances, it would often require additional rater training in order to gain a consensus between raters. There can be grey areas, such as "What constitutes a sentence?" and "What is line regard?" There are often judgments made in a holistic rubric that are not defined by any specific criteria. An instruction sheet with examples should accompany a holistic rubric to assist raters in understanding your expectations and improve the chances of a consensus. Again the same factors that can have an effect on an analytic rubric affect the success of a holistic rubric on generating a consensus. If raters are not absolutely clear on what they are evaluating, the one that suffers is the student.

Chapter Five

Make measurable progress in reasonable time. (Rohn)

Why are Other Staff Members Taking Data on my Goals?

The purpose of staff working on goals that you have written is so that the student will be able to generalize the activity to all situations.

Making Goals Measurable

According to *Writing Measurable Short and Long Term Goals* (KU Writing Center, 2012), "A Measurable Goal is: Quantifiable, Assessable, Computable, Clear, Calculable, Determinate, Finite, And Verifiable." In occupational therapy as well as other health care professions, the acronym RUMBA is used to determine if a goal is measurable and pertinent to the needs of the patient. "RUMBA stands for Relevance, Understandable, Measurable, Behavioral and Attainable" (Contributor, 2013). In educational terms, goals must be measurable and measured. According to (Bateman & Herr, 2010), measurable is a key term or "essential characteristic of the IEP." They go on to state that if a goal is not measurable it cannot be measured and therefore violates IDEA. A rubric, when developed correctly, provides a way to clearly measure goal progress, not only with the therapist but with all evaluators.

The IDEA no longer requires that an IEP include short-term objectives and benchmarks. They are urging that IEP teams continue to use short-term objectives and benchmarks for "compelling educational and legal reasons." Some consider it courting educational, legal and financial disaster to report progress without measurable and measured progress markers. (Bateman & Herr, 2010)

What does Measurable Mean?

Looking up the word *measurable* in the dictionary, the word *quantifiable* appears. Quantifiable implies that there is a numeric component. Can you count how many times the student was actually successful? If you write, "John will write his letters appropriately" does that imply measurability? It really doesn't. Will John form every letter of the alphabet correctly? Will he maintain line regard?

How much is John expected to do? Did you take into account what is expected at his age or grade level? A better and more measurable goal for a very young student might be, "John will form the letters of his first name correctly, without reversals on a sheet of loose-leaf paper in 8/10 trials on 4 consecutive occasions." This is better but we can still make an assumption here. So it might even be better to write "John will form the letters of his first name correctly without visual model with the letter "J" capitalized and all other letters written in lowercase, following line regard and without reversals on a standard sheet of loose-leaf paper in 8/10 trials on 4 consecutive occasions." Using this goal we can then count the letters, how many were capitalized, how many were lowercase, how many times he was able to write on the line and how many letter reversals there were. We can count how many trials he was able to perform correctly and on how many occasions. This is countable and therefore measurable.

Measurable goals are actually quite easy to generate. Parts of a goal include:

- A Given
- Skill or Behavior being addressed
- Method
- Level of Performance
- Time Frame or Criteria Period
- Schedule

You may or may not need to include a *given*. A *given* is something that must be provided to the student in order to achieve his goal. For example: "When provided with a stetro pencil grip [GIVEN], the student will be able to maintain a static tripod grasp when handwriting [SKILL or BEHAVIOR] in 8/10 trials [LEVEL OF PERFORMANCE] over one week [SCHEDULE or CRITERIA PERIOD]." Often a method of assessment is requested as is a schedule of assessment, particularly in IEP data bases. Methods can include things like, recorded observation, checklist and teacher generated materials.

The IDEA is mandating measurability for all students with disabilities. Completing goals, that meet the criteria listed above, attempts to ensure that measurability.

Given	Skill or Behavior	Level of Performance	Criteria Period	Schedule**
When provided with a stetro pencil grip	the student will be able to maintain a static tripod grasp when handwriting	in 8/10 trials	on 4/5 occasions	over one month
It is understood that a computer is to be used and no special equipment is needed.	The student will type at a speed of 30 words per minute with 93% accuracy [less than 3 errors per 30 words]-*try not to use percentages unless you actually calculate what the percentage means, in this case <3 errors.*	In 4/5 trials	on 5 consecutive occasions	In 4 weeks
When provided with a one inch wide wired shoelace	the student will be able to tie his shoe using the double loop method	In 6/10 trials	on 4/5 occasions	in 4 weeks
When provided with small objects [i.e., coins]	the student will be able to demonstrate palm to fingertip translation [bring the coin from the palm to the tip of fingertips] using only one hand and without holding the limb against the body	In 8/10 trials	on 5/5 trials	over 4 weeks

Table 7: Sample Measurable Goals for IEP

**It should be noted that, in general, efficacy of progress markers within the school system is generally assessed every 4 weeks/one month. It is at this time that the rubric or even the goal may need to be modified to ensure a student's success. This is based on the policies of your school district so please ask questions.

Goal Development Chart				
Student:			**School Year:**	
Given	Skill or Behavior	Level of Performance	Criteria Period	Schedule**

Table 8: Goal Development Chart

Chapter Six

"It is a capital mistake to theorize before one has data"

~Sherlock Holmes (Sir Arthur Conan Doyle)

Collecting Relevant Data

"Keep in mind, the term "least restrictive setting," implies that the interventions being used are '**effective**.' Without some form of data collection that gives a reasonable picture of the student's behavior, '**IEP**' meetings often degenerate into a battle of opinions rather than an opportunity to jointly examine objective information. How can measurable, relevant goals and objectives be developed if the underlying information is lacking?" (Gale, 2012) This is quite a powerful statement. Parents, districts and 3rd party payers are becoming more insistent on having good data to support initiation and continuation of services. Reports have to be more informative and describe all the factors that address a particular behavior or skill. Good data is not only a measure of progress but also a reflection on us as therapists. Our goals are supposed to be based on what we know about the student and where we think the student will be in one year from now. Data supports or contradicts our clinical judgments and therefore, potentially, our therapeutic expertise.

Nancy Lowe (2011) stated, "When teachers feel confident and capable of using data …, they unleash the power of data to improve teaching and learning." Occupational therapists, in any setting, are expected to take data on student-client-patient performance leading to effective practice and ultimately evidence-based practice. Formative and summative assessments form a balanced assessment system, as described in Chapter Three. (Garrison & Ehringhaus, 2007)

Formative Data

Data that is collected during occupational therapy session and instructional times [when a teacher or an aide runs your goals] is called *formative data*. This is the data that is used to modify the instructional or in this case therapeutic process to determine how our goals are being met. This data closes the gap between what a student needs to know and what the student has learned. It may appear, when modifying a rubric that we are in some way manipulating what the student needs to learn. That is not the case. We modify the way the student is taught to achieve the end goal. For example: Joey wanted to tie his shoes, due to his inability to get past the initial knot and form loops, the task was modified, based on the formative data collected, so that in the end he was able to tie his shoes successfully. This is a critical thinking, clinical reasoning and clinical judgment process in action. This type of data focuses on the individual in the Individualized Education Plan. (Montgomery Schools) (National Center for Research on Evaluation, Standards, and Student Testing (CRESST))

Summative Data

For a school-based occupational therapist, our summative data is that annual review report that we write each year. This report includes standardized and non-standardized tests, a report of goal progress, clinical observations and possibly assessment rubrics. It is at this time that we report on the progress markers that we have developed. It is this report that helps the Committee on Special Education (CSE) make plans for the student for the coming school year and assess appropriate program placement. (Montgomery Schools; Garrison & Ehringhaus, 2007) Other district and statewide administered assessments are also considered to be summative data. (Lowe, 2011)

Data Collection

"Opinions alone won't cut it anymore. Federal and state mandates like the Individuals with Disabilities Education Improvement Act of 2004 (IDEIA) and No Child Left Behind (NCLB) insist that quantitative assessment of progress become standard practice. It is no longer a choice. Collecting and analyzing data in an objective, quantifiable manner is the law." (Johnston, 2010) As you can see, it is imperative that we, as therapists, collect meaningful data.

As discussed in Chapter Five, goals need to be able to stand on their own without any additional information. In order for data collection to be meaningful, data collection must have a means of consistency from one rater to the next. If another therapist comes in to cover your caseload, that therapist should be able to follow through on your goals seamlessly based on the goals and rubrics that you have created. His or her data should match and build on your data. There should be no guessing whether or not the student has met the criteria for achievement. This should be a black and white area, not room for grey. Did the Joey make two loops without prompts? Yes or No. This is where it is critical for your descriptors to be clear and concise. If your descriptors are not clear and concise, someone is guessing and your data is not meaningful. It is not usable and does not meet the standard practice. Although progress can be recorded through the use of a rubric, in the case of interpreting data, a visual or graph is often optimal for the student, parent and the committee to see the change in behavior (task behavior) that has been achieved using your strategies. "Student record keeping helps students better understand their own learning as evidenced by their classroom work. This process of students keeping ongoing records of their work not only engages students, it also helps them, beyond a "grade," to see where they started and the progress they are making toward the learning goal." (Garrison & Ehringhaus, 2007) In the experience of this author, engaging students in the data collection process not only helps them see the progress they've made but also reduces the stress that they feel as a middle or high school student mandated for occupational therapy services.

Types of Data	
Formative	**Summative**
• Daily Data Collection from Rubrics, Checklists, Task Analysis • Taken during instructional times • Closes the gap between what is known and what needs to be known. • Used to modify therapeutic process	• Standardized Assessment • Statewide Assessments • District Administered Assessments • End of Unit Tests • Used to assess program placement for the coming school year

Table 9: Types of Data

Interpreting Data Worksheet	
Name:	Date:
Goal:	
What does the data suggest about what this student already knows and has learned?	
What does it reveal about this student's ability to apply what has been learned?	
What are this student's strengths with regard to this skill?	
What are this student's weaknesses with regard to this skill?	
Where do you go from here?	

Table 10: Interpreting Data Worksheet

Chapter Seven

Going digital!

Paperless?

This chapter will be written different from any other chapter in this book. The other chapters are written with professional references. This one is written from my own perspective.

Truly, I can be a paper junkie. With all the years in practice, you can imagine how much paper there is or at least was. No more. I can no longer fill the garage with file boxes, drown in paper or rent storage space for files. It is an unrealistic expectation in this day and digital age.

There are many programs out there that are meant for professional therapy clinics. But I needed a program that could work for me. I needed a program that would do the following:

- Maintain my notes in a printable format that looked like an official note or report and not just random notes to jog my memory

- Complete paper work without having to replicate forms each time [templates]

- Be able to use that same format to complete an evaluation, annual review, consult, daily note-taking, without wasting valuable time and effort [templates]

- Something that, if I had to, I could e-mail to one of the agencies through a HIPPA Compliant e-mail service

- Be done with documentation by the end of the therapy session so that I would have time to spend with my family and not waste hours per day catching up and trying to remember.

- The option to have my client/student sign-in and not have to carry additional paperwork

- Be able to create my own system of organization

- Be able to easily import pertinent e-mails and documents from other sources [prescriptions, outside reports, follow ups, etc.]

I looked at a number of note-taking and clinical documentation programs and I found that I already had programming on my computer that would work for me. I use Microsoft OneNote. I didn't really need the billing components since I already have that so I did not have to order another subscription to a clinically based program.

I carry a large purse. In that purse, I carry the typical girl supplies, and a mini-laptop, a handheld scanner and a Bamboo [pen tablet]. I am not a fan of the iPad, I am a PC girl! Since I am a 'cash-based practice,' I carry my tiny credit card reader for those clients wanting to pay using a credit card. I could do all that with an iPad, it's true, I just prefer my PC.

I can create assessment rubrics in MS OneNote and save them as a template. That way, I never have to worry about typing over the rubric and losing the original, having to do it all over again. Saving a document as a template is easy in OneNote as it is a feature of the 'New Page' tab. I also like using OneNote to keep my clients engaged in their progress. As we go through the task that the rubric was designed for, I have my clients click the box on their level of progress for a particular criterion. I add as many templates as I like to a client's notebook. I can add date and time with just a click [for entering and exiting a client's home]. My notes are done on the spot. I can even sign my notes and have my client sign using my Bamboo and send them off along with the invoice using a HIPPA Compliant e-mail system, if I need to. It can't be easier than that! You never have to worry about carrying multiple file folders again.

I create a notebook for each client. The templates are available across all notebooks. I never need to recreate a template for another notebook. This is a real time saver. If I need to modify a rubric for an individual client, I just modify it, resave it as a new template and use the new template for that client. This does mean that you have to be good at pre-planning, but you would need to do that if you were using paper and pen, as well.

I like to use Excel to monitor my client's progress, as you will see in the case study for Charlotte, later in this book. Excel allows me to create a chart for progress providing a visual representation. This is so much better during a CSE meeting or even a meeting with the client, his or her family or even reporting to a physician. The chart can be inserted into your report in a matter of seconds. I engage my students by having them enter the data as part of the therapy session. My students like to see how close they are to achieving their goals. Many of my students are older [middle and high school], and wanting to be done with therapy. Their involvement keeps them coming back just to see progress and accomplishment.

The last thing you should know is that this type of programming can also be used for evaluations. I use a number of rubrics in my evaluations [i.e., keyboarding, handwriting, etc.]. I also use *The Student Interview* and have a version in OneNote. If the student is able to complete the interview independently, I set them up on the computer and allow them to complete the document in OneNote. I have to say that the interview is completed very quickly, once the student understands how to use OneNote. Evaluations, rubrics, and notes can be printed directly from OneNote, if needed. I have done that in a pinch when a district has asked for an evaluation on the day of a CSE Meeting. You know, one of those 'oops!' we forgot to request the evaluation. Can you do it today? Microsoft OneNote has saved the day on many an occasion.

Lastly, I have developed rubrics that incorporate pictures for students in need. I never have to worry about making copies or copies from copies that become illegible over time. I always have a fresh one ready to go. I don't waste money on ink or paper. I never have to carry around a heavy bag with file folders filled with notes.

Creating a template is relatively easy in OneNote 2010. There is a tiny downward arrow next to 'new page' in the 'new page' tab. Click on that little downward arrow and up pops a little menu. At the bottom of that menu, click on 'Page Templates.' Once you click there, at the very bottom of the column is what you need, 'Save current page as template.' Name the template and that is all there is to it. If you make changes, the program will ask you to rename the template. If you name it with the same name, of course, you will make changes to the original template. All the documents created previously will not change, only the documents going forward. As you can see, in my rubrics, I have created templates with check boxes for easy scoring. You can use the same template over and over and never worry about wasting paper or your rubric being illegible. You can even add photos if you need to.

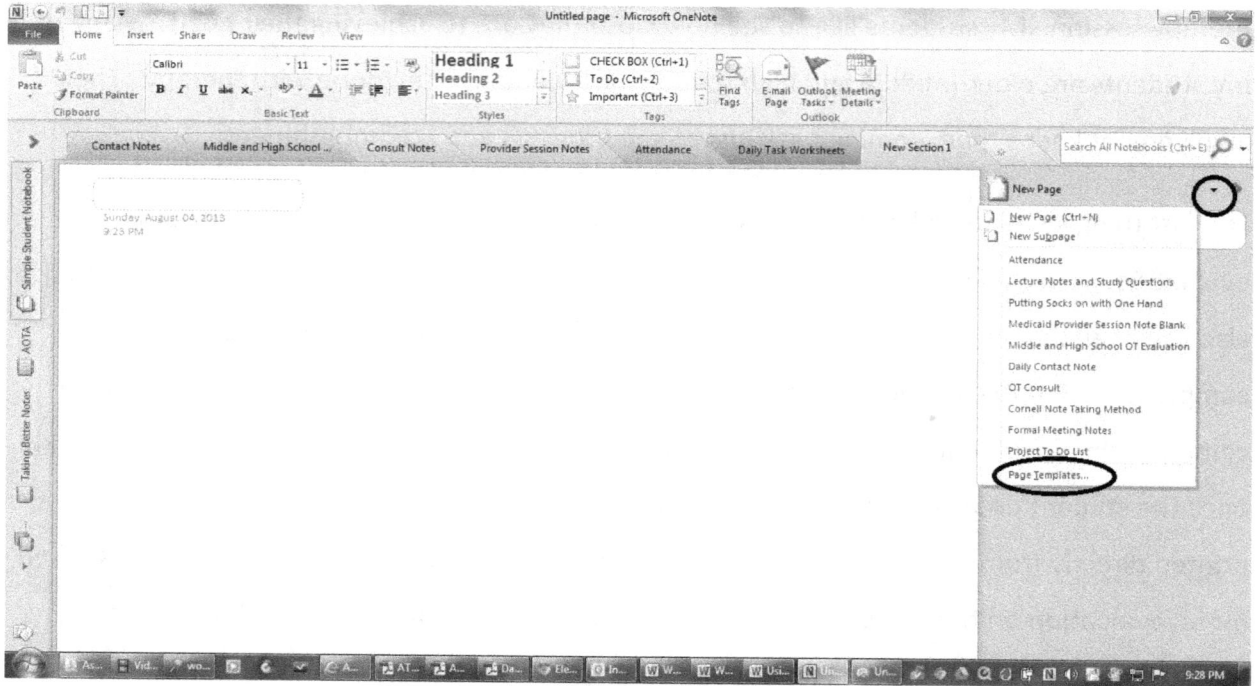

Figure 2: Creating a template in Microsoft OneNote 2010

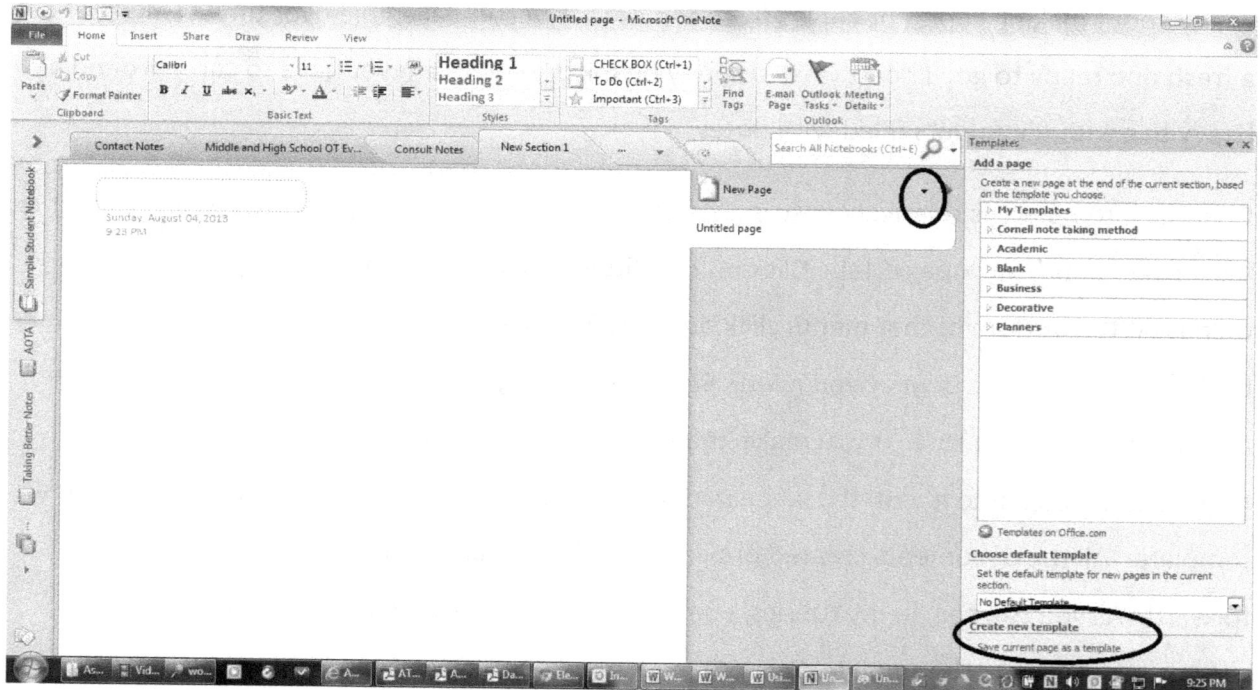

Figure 3: Saving as a template in Microsoft OneNote 2010

Chapter Eight

A process of investigation

Case Studies

A case study is a detailed account of the student/client/patient. In this case, the two cases included, studies give us a look at how an assessment rubric is used to make an initial assessment of a particular skill. Later a rubric was also used to monitor progress. Sometimes, the same rubric can be used to motor progress that was used to assess the skill initially. Other times, a new rubric needs to be developed, particularly when a task needs to be adapted in order for the student to be successful. This can be confusing. We are not changing data to make the student appear successful. Occupational therapists are skilled in adapting or modifying tasks to help students become successful as you will see with Joey.

Joey

Joey was about 12 years old and in his first year in middle school. Joey was diagnosed with Autism and indicated, by doing, that he wanted to be independent in a number of self-care skills. Joey had significant speech delays. He often expressed his wants and needs by trying to perform a task independently. He would retrieve some of the necessary items, independently. Unfortunately, this often met with negative responses, "Joey, do you want to…? You need to ask. Please put the [supplies] back. Take a seat and ask." While this was an attempt to have him verbalized and follow classroom rules; it was very frustrating for him to be denied the opportunities he was seeking. Joey seemed to want to tie his shoes. Each time his shoe became untied, he would attempt to tie it. There were many occupational therapists that had come before; none of whom were successful in helping him learn a skill that he desired. Joey was a perseverative knotter. As hard as he tried, he was stuck in a pattern of making knots but could never get to make the loops and subsequently the bow.

The shoe tying assessment was completed with a rubric developed for the double loop method. The double loop method was chosen because of his perseveration with knots. It is a simple process of a single knot, then make two loops, make a knot with the loops and then there is a bow.

Task: Shoe Tying

Plan: Assessment

Initially the plan was to collect data on shoe tying using the double loop method during 3 consecutive therapy sessions. As previously reported, Joey perseverated on tying the knots. With hand over hand assistance, Joey was able to make loops and form a bow.

Data collection continued for 3 days using the Double Loop Method of Shoe Tying Assessment Rubric to determine if Joey consistently perseverated in the same place by at least one other rater. Related service goals were run twice per day in his classroom by his aide and teacher in addition to the ones carried out during treatment sessions. Therefore data was taken on 8 occasions by three raters.

1. The Double Loop Method Shoe Tying Assessment Rubric is based on the book Red Lace Yellow Lace (Casey, Herbst, & Stanley, 1996) and used as a visual prompt and shoe model. It was provided to the classroom staff along with the rubric. However, the rubric does not refer to the colors of the shoe lace.
2. The teacher and aide were in-serviced to use the rubric and collect data

Questions & Answers:

1. What is his present level of performance in shoe tying?
    a. Joey was not able to bring the tips of the lace together equalize the length of both ends of the shoe lace
    b. Joey was able to make the first knot by crossing the ends of the shoe lace fold one lace over the other, insert it into the space then pull to create the knot.
    c. Joey was unable to form loops. He did not know where to grasp the lace to create the loop and subsequently reverted to perseverative knotting.
2. What method of shoe tying should he be taught?
    a. Joey's ability to form knots appeared perseverative but was actually one of his strengths and the double loop method was chosen
3. What is interfering with his ability to tie shoes?
    a. Joey may have been perseverating on knots because he could not figure out how to achieve the next step and form a loop.

4. Can I build on any skills that he currently has?

    a. Since knotting was a strength, a knot was placed at the point of finger placement to form the loops. Joey was prompted with the phrase, "Tie your shoes."

        i. This continued to result in perseverative knotting.

5. Should I adapt a shoe tying method to help him be successful? And how?

    a. The initial prompt was changed to "Pinch the knots to tie your shoes. "The initial knot was eliminated to prevent the serial or perseverative knotting.

    b. This resulted in Joey making the loops first, and then making a knot with the loops. Immediate success! A second knot was required to secure the bow and Joey was successful. He continued to be successful as long as the prompt began with "Pinch the knots..." If prompted, "Tie your shoes," Joey reverted back to perseverative knotting.

Results & Follow Up:

Joey continued to be successful and achieved mastery of the task within days using the amended prompt. His ability to perform the task remained consistent. The following year, Joey had a different occupational therapist. She prompted him with "Tie your shoe" and the same perseverative knotting appeared. We later discussed this as she stated he was not able to tie his shoes. I asked if she minded if I intervened and she agreed. I knotted Joey's shoe laces at the apex of the loop, prompted him to "Pinch the knots to tie your shoes." Joey performed the shoe typing task without further prompting. It should be noted that a video was made during initial training to support Joey's progress and was sent home to the parent for follow through over the summer months.

Double Loop Shoe Tying Assessment Rubric

Name:		Date Initiated:		
		Date Ended:		
Prompt	*'Tie your shoes'*	□ *Student's shoe placed on table top* □ *Student is wearing his shoe*		
Criteria	**1**	**2**	**3**	**4**
Equalize Shoe Lace Length	Student requires physical assistance to equalize the length of the loose ends of the shoe lace	Student requires demonstration, picture and verbal prompts to	Student requires no more than 2 prompts □ demonstration □ verbal □ picture prompt to	Without demonstration, picture prompts, or verbal cues student was able to equalize the length of the shoe laces.
Cross Laces [Make an 'X']	Student requires physical assistance to cross the laces	Student requires demonstration, picture and verbal prompts to cross the laces	Student requires no more than 2 prompts □ demonstration □ verbal □ picture prompt to cross the laces	Without demonstration, picture prompts, or verbal cues student was able to cross the laces
Fold one lace over the other	Student requires physical assistance to fold one lace over the other	Student requires demonstration, picture and verbal prompts to fold one lace over the other	Student requires no more than 2 prompts □ demonstration □ verbal □ picture prompt to fold one lace over the other	Without demonstration, picture prompts, or verbal cues student was able to fold one lace over the other
Push the lace through the lower space	Student requires physical assistance to push the lace through the lower space	Student requires demonstration, picture and verbal prompts to push the lace through the lower space	Student requires no more than 2 prompts □ demonstration □ verbal □ picture prompt to push the lace through the lower space	Without demonstration, picture prompts, or verbal cues student was able to push the lace through the lower space
Pull tight	Student requires physical assistance to pull the laces tight	Student requires demonstration, picture and verbal prompts to pull the laces tight	Student requires no more than 2 prompts □ demonstration □ verbal □ picture prompt to pull the laces tight	Without demonstration, picture prompts, or verbal cues student was able to pull the laces tight
Make two loops	Student requires physical assistance to make two loops	Student requires demonstration, picture and verbal prompts to make two loops	Student requires no more than 2 prompts □ demonstration □ verbal □ picture prompt to make two loops	Without demonstration, picture prompts, or verbal cues student was able to make two loops
Cross the loops [Make an 'X']	Student requires physical assistance to cross the loops	Student requires demonstration, picture and verbal prompts to cross the loops	Student requires no more than 2 prompts □ demonstration □ verbal □ picture prompt to cross the loops	Without demonstration, picture prompts, or verbal cues student was able to cross the loops
Fold one lace over the other	Student requires physical assistance to fold one lace over the other	Student requires demonstration, picture and verbal prompts to fold one lace over the other	Student requires no more than 2 prompts □ demonstration □ verbal □ picture prompt to fold one lace over the other	Without demonstration, picture prompts, or verbal cues student was able to fold one lace over the other
Push the loop through the lower space	Student requires physical assistance to push the loop through the lower space	Student requires demonstration, picture and verbal prompts to push the loop through the lower space	Student requires no more than 2 prompts □ demonstration □ verbal □ picture prompt to push the loop through the lower space	Without demonstration, picture prompts, or verbal cues student was able to push the loop through the lower space
Pull tight the loops tight to make a bow	Student requires physical assistance to pull tight the loops tight to make a bow	Student requires demonstration, picture and verbal prompts to pull tight the loops tight to make a bow	Student requires no more than 2 prompts □ demonstration □ verbal pull tight the loops tight to make a bow	Without demonstration, picture prompts, or verbal cues student was able to pull tight the loops tight to make a bow

Table 11: Double Loop Shoe Tying Assessment Rubric

Double Loop Shoe Tying Assessment Data Sheet					
Name:			**Date Initiated:**		
			Date Ended:		
	Monday	**Tuesday**	**Wednesday**	**Thursday**	**Friday**
Criteria	**Score** / **# Prompts**	**Score** / **# Prompts**	**Score** / **# Prompts**	**Score** / **# Prompts**	**Score** / **# Prompts**
Equalize Shoe Lace Length					
Cross Laces [Make an 'X']					
Fold one lace over the other					
Push the lace through the lower space					
Pull tight					
Make two loops					
Cross the loops [Make an 'X']					
Fold one lace over the other					
Push the loop through the lower space					
Pull tight the loops tight to make a bow					
Date:	**Comments:**				

Table 12: Double Loop Shoe Tying Assessment Data Sheet

Adapted Double Loop Shoe Tying Rubric

Name:		Date Initiated:		
		Date Ended:		
Prompt	*'Pinch the knots to tie your shoes'*	☐ *Student's shoe placed on table top* ☐ *Student is wearing his shoe*		
Criteria	**1**	**2**	**3**	**4**
Pinch the knots	Student requires physical assistance to pinch the knots	Student requires demonstration, picture and verbal prompts to pinch the knots	Student requires no more than 2 prompts ☐ demonstration ☐ verbal ☐ picture prompt to pinch the knots	Without demonstration, picture prompts, or verbal cues student was able to pinch the knots
Make two loops	Student requires physical assistance to make two loops	Student requires demonstration, picture and verbal prompts to make two loops	Student requires no more than 2 prompts ☐ demonstration ☐ verbal ☐ picture prompt to make two loops	Without demonstration, picture prompts, or verbal cues student was able to make two loops
Fold one loop over the other	Student requires physical assistance to fold one loop over the other	Student requires demonstration, picture and verbal prompts to fold one loop over the other	Student requires no more than 2 prompts ☐ demonstration ☐ verbal ☐ picture prompt to fold one loop over the other	Without demonstration, picture prompts, or verbal cues student was able to fold one loop over the other
Go through the lower space	Student requires physical assistance to push the loop through the lower space	Student requires demonstration, picture and verbal prompts to push the loop through the lower space	Student requires no more than 2 prompts ☐ demonstration ☐ verbal ☐ picture prompt to push the loop through the lower space	Without demonstration, picture prompts, or verbal cues student was able to push the loop through the lower space
Pull the loops	Student requires physical assistance to pull the loops tight	Student requires demonstration, picture and verbal prompts to pull the loops tight	Student requires no more than 2 prompts ☐ demonstration ☐ verbal ☐ picture prompt to pull the loops tight	Without demonstration, picture prompts, or verbal cues student was able to pull the loops tight
Hold the loops	Student requires physical assistance to hold the loops	Student requires demonstration, picture and verbal prompts to make hold the loops	Student requires no more than 2 prompts ☐ demonstration ☐ verbal ☐ picture prompt to hold the loops	Without demonstration, picture prompts, or verbal cues student was able to hold the loops
Fold one loop over the other	Student requires physical assistance to fold one loop over the other	Student requires demonstration, picture and verbal prompts to fold one loop over the other	Student requires no more than 2 prompts ☐ demonstration ☐ verbal ☐ picture prompt to fold one loop over the other	Without demonstration, picture prompts, or verbal cues student was able to fold one loop over the other
Go through the lower space	Student requires physical assistance to push the loop through the lower space	Student requires demonstration, picture and verbal prompts to push the loop through the lower space	Student requires no more than 2 prompts ☐ demonstration ☐ verbal ☐ picture prompt to push the loop through the lower space	Without demonstration, picture prompts, or verbal cues student was able to push the loop through the lower space
Pull the loops	Student requires physical assistance to pull the loops tight	Student requires demonstration, picture and verbal prompts to pull the loops tight	Student requires no more than 2 prompts ☐ demonstration ☐ verbal ☐ picture prompt to pull the loops tight	Without demonstration, picture prompts, or verbal cues student was able to pull the loops tight and complete the bow.

Table 13: Adapted Double Loop Shoe Tying Rubric

Adapted Double Loop Shoe Tying Assessment Rubric Data Collection Sheet

Name:			Date Initiated:		
			Date Ended:		
	Monday	**Tuesday**	**Wednesday**	**Thursday**	**Friday**
Criteria	**Score** / **# Prompts**	**Score** / **# Prompts**	**Score** / **# Prompts**	**Score** / **# Prompts**	**Score** / **# Prompts**
Pinch the knots					
Make two loops					
Fold one loop over the other					
Go through the lower space					
Pull the loops					
Hold the loops					
Fold one loop over the other					
Go through the lower space					
Pull the loops					
Pinch the knots					
Date:	**Comments:**				

Table 14: Adapted Double Loop Shoe Tying Assessment Rubric Data Collection Sheet

Charlotte

Charlotte was a 6th grade student with a congenital amputation of the right upper extremity mid-humerus. She was in regular and advanced placement classes undergoing a private occupational therapy evaluation for keyboarding, energy conservation and modification of educationally relevant fine motor tasks. The parent was concerned about her ability to maintain pace with her peers and the potential for injury due to strain on the existing limb. This evaluation would be discussed at a 504 conference as part of an annual review. Standardized and non-standardized was conducted to meet the needs of educational process. In all tests and subtests, Charlotte scored in the average to above average range. Her handwriting was considered to be excellent. She was able to keep pace with her peers, with legible handwriting, good spacing, letter formation and line regard. With a binder, a loose-leaf pad attached to a clip board and four small squares of Dycem attached to both the back of the binder and the clipboard, Charlotte was quite proficient in handwriting. She appeared to be well organized, used her agenda appropriately, never missed an assignment and could locate her work when asked without difficulty. An aide helped her pack her backpack at the end of the day. She used a wheeled backpack due to its weight. Since Charlotte was able to use only one hand for keyboarding, the Keyboarding Rubric was slightly modified to account for her physical disability. She was assessed using a rubric developed specifically for her situation based on Lily Walters One-Hand Typing Program. (Walters, 2002-2013)

Task: Keyboarding

The parent specifically requested an assessment of keyboarding skills and stated that the results of this assessment would be shared with the school district.

Plan: Assessment

To assess her present level of performance in keyboarding, develop an assessment rubric based on the skill of one-hand typing. The Keyboarding Assessment Rubric was appropriate for the situation with one minor change. The positioning of the keyboard was changed from" Center of the body (belly button) aligned with the letter "H" on Keyboard" to "Keyboard is positioned slightly off midline toward the unaffected side of the body." Posture was assessed in both sitting and standing. Very slight curvature to the left was noted. Muscle strength and muscle tone was considered to be within normal limits in all planes of motion throughout the shoulders, scapulars and left upper extremity. Charlotte was able to perform all self-care tasks

Questions & Answers:

1. What previous experience did Charlotte have with the computer and keyboard?
   a. Charlotte has had some experience with the computer both at home and in her core classes. She has not had formal training in keyboarding.

2. How will her deficits affect her keyboarding skills?
   a. She will be keyboarding with her left hand only. She does not have the ability to use her right residual limb to support keyboarding due to limb length.
   b. Her home row keys are now "F-G-H-J" and not the typical "A-S-D-F/:-L-K-J."
   c. Postural control and keyboard placement are critical in terms of maintaining stamina, supporting hand placement and achieving good accuracy.. Keyboarding placement needs to shift to the left ["H" aligned with the left elbow] to reduce fatigue and potential errors.

Results & Follow Up:

Charlotte was seen privately for 3 months to work on keyboarding skills. A goal of typing at a rate of 25 words per minute with two errors with a one hand touch typing method within 3 months was recommended. To follow through on the exercise program performed in therapy sessions, Charlotte and her parents were provided with a home exercise program to support postural control along with upper extremity muscle strength. Within one month of consistent practice at home and in therapy sessions, Charlotte typing speed was increasing steadily achieving a rate of 18 with one error. The same assessment used for evaluation was used to monitor her progress. No changes needed to be made. She quickly and consistently achieved scores of 3 and 4 in all criteria resulting in marked improvement in her overall typing speed and accuracy.

Student's Name:			Date Assessed:			
One Handed Keyboarding Assessment						
		Period:	WPM goal:	# in Group:	Time Allowed:	Score
	SCORE	1	2	3	4	
CONTROL OF BODY	POSTURE	Keyboard is positioned slightly off midline toward the unaffected side of the body	And feet flat on the floor with a straight back	And elbows at the side with wrists positioned off the key board	And fingers curved over the home row.	
	ATTENTION	Eyes on screen or copy and typed <25% of the time	Eyes on screen or copy and typed 25-50% of the time	Eyes on screen or copy and typed 50-75% of the time	Eyes on screen or copy and typed 75-100% of the time	
	TOUCH TYPING	Used the correct fingers on the keys <25% of the time	Used the correct fingers on the keys 25-50% of the time	Used the correct fingers on the keys 50-75% of the time	Used the correct fingers on the keys 100% of the time	
	WORDS PER MINUTE	Achieved <25% of the WPM Goal	Achieved 25-50% of the WPM Goal	Achieved 50-75% of the WPM Goal	Achieved 75-100% of the WPM Goal	
TASK BEHAVIOR	NUMBER OF MINUTES TO BEGIN TASK	More than 4 minutes	3-4 minutes	2-3 minutes	1 minute or less	
	NUMBER OF REQUESTED ASSISTS	More than 3 requests for assistance without seeking assistance from a peer	2-3 requests for assistance without seeking assistance from a peer	1-2 requests for assistance without seeking assistance from a peer	Did not seek assistance from teacher/therapist	
	TIME ON TASK	Required 3 or more prompts to remain on typing task.	Required 2-3 prompts to remain on typing task	Required 1-2 prompt to remain on typing task	Required 0 prompts to remain on typing task	
	PERCENTAGE OF TYPING TASK COMPLETED	Completed <25% of the task within the time allowed	Completed 25-50% of the task within the time allowed	Completed 25-75% of the task within the time allowed	Completed 75-100% of the task within the time allowed	
BASIC PROGRAM KNOWLEDGE	FORMAT DOCUMENT (Margins, title, name, date, justification, bold, underline, font and spacing, etc.)	After identification of document style (i.e., business letter, essay, etc.), completed page set up with written directions and 2 or more prompts	After identification of document style (i.e., business letter, essay, etc.), completed page set up with written directions and 1 prompt	After identification of document style (i.e., business letter, essay, etc.), completed page set up with written directions	After identification of document style (i.e., business letter, essay, etc.), completed page set up independently	
	USE OF PROGRAM FEATURES (Spellcheck, grammar check, cut & paste, graphics, etc.)	After prior instruction the student is able to use program features as required by the assignment with 3 or more prompts	After prior instruction the student is able to use program features as required by the assignment with 2-2 prompts	After prior instruction the student is able to use program features as required by the assignment with 1-2 prompts	After prior instruction the student is able to use program features as required by the assignment without prompts	

Comments/Observations: Check One: ☐ Initial Assessment   ☐ Follow Up

Table 15: One Hand Keyboarding Assessment

Date	Actual WPM	Goal WPM	Errors
9/26/2012	10	25	3
10/1/2012	12	25	2
10/4/2012	11	25	2
10/8/2012	14	25	2
10/12/2012	15	25	1
10/15/2012	17	25	1
10/17/2012	16	25	2
10/20/2012	18	25	1

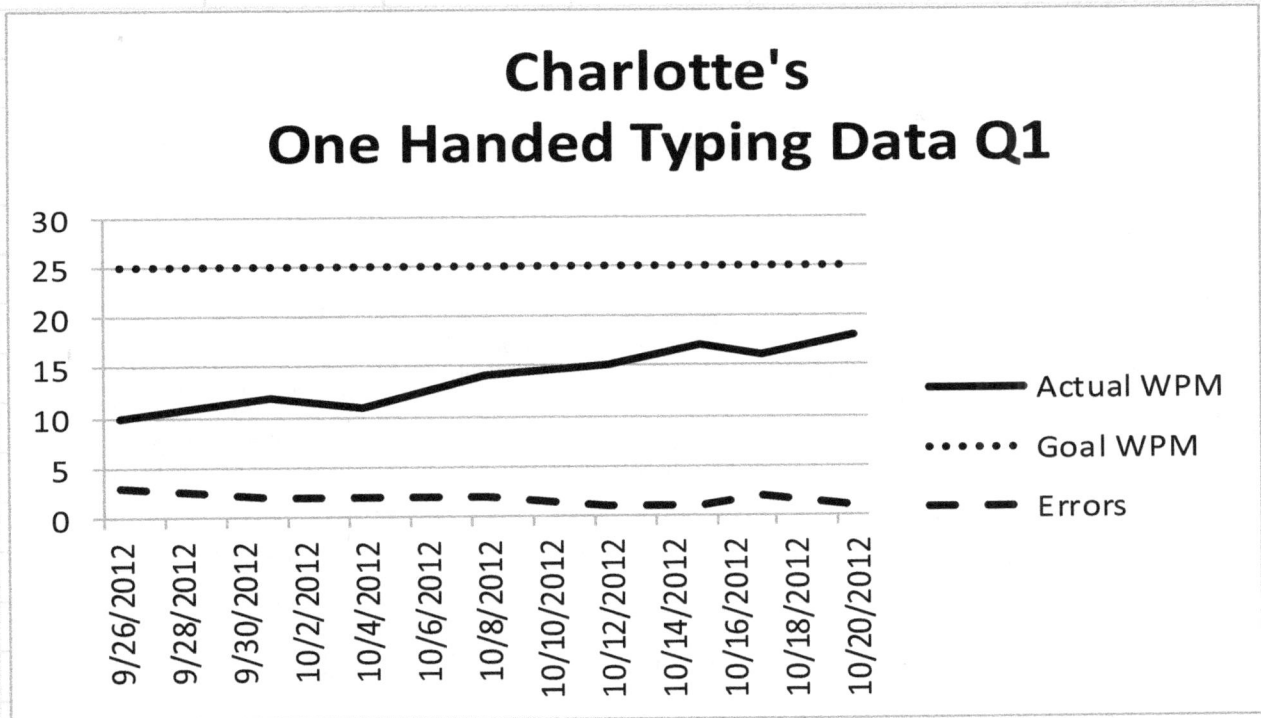

Charlotte's One Handed Typing Data Q1

Table 16: Graphic Representation of Data Collected

As you can see the visual representation of the data collected on Charlotte's typing speed, clearly indicates that she has made great strides in achieving her goals. This kind of visual makes "data at a glance" possible.

Keyboarding Assessment Rubric						
Student's Name:				Date Assessed:		
		Period:	WPM goal:	# in Group:	Time Allowed:	Score
	SCORE	1	2	3	4	
CONTROL OF BODY	POSTURE	Center of the body (belly button) aligned with the letter "H" on Keyboard	And feet flat on the floor with a straight back	And elbows at the side with wrists positioned off the key board	And fingers curved over the home row.	
	ATTENTION	Eyes on screen or copy and typed <25% of the time	Eyes on screen or copy and typed 25-50% of the time	Eyes on screen or copy and typed 50-75% of the time	Eyes on screen or copy and typed 75-100% of the time	
	TOUCH TYPING	Used the correct fingers on the keys <25% of the time	Used the correct fingers on the keys 25-50% of the time	Used the correct fingers on the keys 50-75% of the time	Used the correct fingers on the keys 100% of the time	
	WORDS PER MINUTE	Achieved <25% of the WPM Goal	Achieved 25-50% of the WPM Goal	Achieved 50-75% of the WPM Goal	Achieved 75-100% of the WPM Goal	
TASK BEHAVIOR	NUMBER OF MINUTES TO BEGIN TASK	More than 4 minutes	3-4 minutes	2-3 minutes	1 minute or less	
	NUMBER OF REQUESTED ASSISTS	More than 3 requests for assistance without seeking assistance from a peer	2-3 requests for assistance without seeking assistance from a peer	1-2 requests for assistance without seeking assistance from a peer	Did not seek assistance from teacher/therapist	
	TIME ON TASK	Required 3 or more prompts to remain on typing task.	Required 2-3 prompts to remain on typing task	Required 1-2 prompt to remain on typing task	Required 0 prompts to remain on typing task	
	PERCENTAGE OF TYPING TASK COMPLETED	Completed <25% of the task within the time allowed	Completed 25-50% of the task within the time allowed	Completed 25-75% of the task within the time allowed	Completed 75-100% of the task within the time allowed	
BASIC PROGRAM KNOWLEDGE	FORMAT DOCUMENT (Margins, title, name, date, justification, bold, underline, font and spacing, etc.)	After identification of document style (i.e., business letter, essay, etc.), completed page set up with written directions and 2 or more prompts	After identification of document style (i.e., business letter, essay, etc.), completed page set up with written directions and 1 prompt	After identification of document style (i.e., business letter, essay, etc.), completed page set up with written directions	After identification of document style (i.e., business letter, essay, etc.), completed page set up independently	
	USE OF PROGRAM FEATURES (Spellcheck, grammar check, cut & paste, graphics, etc.)	After prior instruction the student is able to use program features as required by the assignment with 3 or more prompts	After prior instruction the student is able to use program features as required by the assignment with 2-2 prompts	After prior instruction the student is able to use program features as required by the assignment with 1-2 prompts	After prior instruction the student is able to use program features as required by the assignment without prompts	

Comments/Observations: Check One: ☐ Initial Assessment   ☐ Follow Up

Table 17: Keyboarding Assessment Rubric

Patient:		Date Initiated:		Date Completed:
Primary Therapist:		Affected Side:		
Diagnoses:				

Assessment Rubric: Putting on Socks with One Hand

Directions: Score the patient's performance on each level of the task. If the patient is not able to complete any portion of the level, the patient scores "0" for that level. Notice the measurement is in the number of trials achieved and is not measured by percentage of time, which can be subjective. A patient may achieve a different score for each portion or criteria of a task so that this rubric contains checklists to measure differences.

	Criteria	Score 1: [<2/5 trials] □ With prompts	Score 2: [3/5 trials] □ With prompts	Score 3: [4/5 trials] □ With prompts	Score 4: [5/5 trial] must be w/o prompts
1	Sit in a firm chair or the side of the bed. If sitting in a wheelchair, lock all the wheels. Have the footrests up and your feet on the floor.	□ Maintain static sitting balance □ Locks W/C wheels □ Footrests elevated □ Feet flat on floor	□ Maintain static sitting balance □ Locks W/C wheels □ Footrests elevated □ Feet flat on floor	□ Maintain static sitting balance □ Locks W/C wheels □ Footrests elevated □ Feet flat on floor	□ Maintain static sitting balance □ Locks W/C wheels □ Footrests elevated □ Feet flat on floor
2	Use the strong hand to reach and grab the ankle of the weak leg. Cross the weak leg over your strong leg.	□ Maintain dynamic sitting balance when reaching for L.E. □ Grasps ankle □ Crosses one leg over the other	□ Maintain dynamic sitting balance when reaching for L.E. □ Grasps ankle □ Crosses one leg over the other	□ Maintain dynamic sitting balance when reaching for L.E. □ Grasps ankle □ Crosses one leg over the other	□ Maintain dynamic sitting balance when reaching for L.E. □ Grasps ankle □ Crosses one leg over the other
3	Place the sock on your lap with the opening of the sock towards your hand.	□ Places sock on lap □ Oriented toward hand	□ Places sock on lap □ Oriented toward hand	□ Places sock on lap □ Oriented toward hand	□ Places sock on lap □ Oriented toward hand
4	Bring fingertips together and place them inside the opening of the sock	□ Brings fingertips together □ Places fingertips inside sock	□ Brings fingertips together □ Places fingertips inside sock	□ Brings fingertips together □ Places fingertips inside sock	□ Brings fingertips together □ Places fingertips inside sock
5	Push fingers into the sock so the second knuckles are in the sock and spread your fingers and thumb out	□ Pushes fingers into sock past the second knuckle □ Spreads fingers and thumb out	□ Pushes fingers into sock past the second knuckle □ Spreads fingers and thumb out	□ Pushes fingers into sock past the second knuckle □ Spreads fingers and thumb out	□ Pushes fingers into sock past the second knuckle □ Spreads fingers and thumb out
6	Leans forward and places the opening of the sock over all the toes. Making sure all the fingers are inside of the sock opening.	□ Maintains dynamic sitting balance when reaching forward □ Places sock over toes □ Keeps fingers inside sock	□ Maintains dynamic sitting balance when reaching forward □ Places sock over toes □ Keeps fingers inside sock	□ Maintains dynamic sitting balance when reaching forward □ Places sock over toes □ Keeps fingers inside sock	□ Maintains dynamic sitting balance when reaching forward □ Places sock over toes □ Keeps fingers inside sock
7	When the sock is over all the toes, the sock is pulled over the rest of the foot.	□ Sock is pulled over the rest of the foot.	□ Sock is pulled over the rest of the foot	□ Sock is pulled over the rest of the foot	□ Sock is pulled over the rest of the foot
8	Uncross the legs.	□ Uncrosses Legs	□ Uncrosses Legs	□ Uncrosses Legs	□ Uncrosses Legs

Table 18: Assessment Rubric: Putting on Socks with One Hand

Patient:		Date Initiated:				Date Completed:									
Data Collection: Putting on Socks with One Hand		Monday		Tuesday		Wednesday		Thursday		Friday		Saturday		Sunday	
		Date:		Date:		Date:		Date:		Date:		Date:		Date:	
Criteria		Right	Left	Right	Left	Right	Left	Right	Left	Right	Left	Right	Left	Right	Left
1	Sit in a firm chair or the side of the bed. If sitting in a wheelchair, lock all the wheels. Have the footrests up and your feet on the floor.	□ Maintain static sitting balance □ Locks W/C wheels □ Footrests elevated □ Feet flat on floor													
2	Use the strong hand to reach and grab the ankle of the weak leg. Cross the weak leg over your strong leg.	□ Maintain dynamic sitting balance when reaching for L.E. □ Grasps ankle □ Crosses one leg over the other													
3	Place the sock on your lap with the opening of the sock towards your hand.	□ Places sock on lap □ Oriented toward hand													
4	Bring fingertips together and place them inside the opening of the sock	□ Brings fingertips together □ Places fingertips inside sock													
5	Push fingers into the sock so the second knuckles are in the sock and spread your fingers and thumb out	□ Pushes fingers into sock past the second knuckle □ Spreads fingers and thumb out													
6	Leans forward and places the opening of the sock over all the toes. Making sure all the fingers are inside of the sock opening.	□ Maintains dynamic sitting balance when reaching forward □ Places sock over toes □ Keeps fingers inside sock													
7	When the sock is over all the toes, the sock is pulled over the rest of the foot.	□ Sock is pulled over the rest of the foot.													
8	Uncross the legs.	□ Uncrosses Legs													
Signature/Primary:		Initials		Initials		Initials		Initials		Initials		Initials		Initials	
Signature/Covering:		Initials		Initials		Initials		Initials		Initials		Initials		Initials	
Signature/Covering:		Initials		Initials		Initials		Initials		Initials		Initials		Initials	

Table 19: Data Collection: Putting on Socks with One Hand

Student:		Date Initiated:		Date Completed:
Therapist:		Teacher:		
Grade:	School Year:		Week Beginning:	

Assessment Rubric: Packaging Utensils

Directions: Student will gather materials [bins, knives, forks, spoons and napkins] and complete the task based on goal criteria. Student must grasp and place the items in the correct sequence. If the student does not follow the correct sequence, the task must be restarted from the beginning Prompt: V=Verbal; VS=Visual; G=Gestural; P=Physical

	Criteria	Score 1:	Score 2:	Score 3:	Score 4:
1	Upon request, student will gather all materials [10 of each]	□ <2/5 trials □ With prompts	□ 3/5 trials □ With prompts	□ 4/5 trials □ With prompts	□ 5/5 trial must be w/o prompts
2	Student will use pincer grasp to grasp the napkin and then unfold it	□ <2/5 trials □ With prompts	□ 3/5 trials □ With prompts	□ 4/5 trials □ With prompts	□ 5/5 trial must be w/o prompts
3	Student will use a pincer grasp to grasp and place the spoon on the napkin	□ <2/5 trials □ With prompts	□ 3/5 trials □ With prompts	□ 4/5 trials □ With prompts	□ 5/5 trial must be w/o prompts
4	Student will use a pincer grasp to grasp and place the fork on the napkin	□ <2/5 trials □ With prompts	□ 3/5 trials □ With prompts	□ 4/5 trials □ With prompts	□ 5/5 trial must be w/o prompts
5	Student will a pincer grasp to grasp and place the knife on the napkin	□ <2/5 trials □ With prompts	□ 3/5 trials □ With prompts	□ 4/5 trials □ With prompts	□ 5/5 trial must be w/o prompts
6	Student will tightly roll the napkin around the utensils	□ <2/5 trials □ With prompts	□ 3/5 trials □ With prompts	□ 4/5 trials □ With prompts	□ 5/5 trial must be w/o prompts
7	Student will place the completed package in the correct bin.	□ <2/5 trials □ With prompts	□ 3/5 trials □ With prompts	□ 4/5 trials □ With prompts	□ 5/5 trial must be w/o prompts
8	Student will return the bin with the packaged utensils to the correct location	□ <2/5 trials □ With prompts	□ 3/5 trials □ With prompts	□ 4/5 trials □ With prompts	□ 5/5 trial must be w/o prompts

Data Collection Week of	Monday			Tuesday			Wednesday			Thursday			Friday		
Criteria	Trials	# Prompt	Type	Trials	# Prompt	Type	Trials	# Prompt	Type	Trials	# Prompt	Type	Trials	# Prompt	Type
1. Upon request, student will gather all materials [10 of each]															
2. Student will use pincer grasp to grasp the napkin and then unfold it															
3. Student will use a pincer grasp to grasp and place the spoon on the napkin															
4. Student will use a pincer grasp to grasp and place the fork on the napkin															
5. Student will use a pincer grasp to grasp and place the knife on the napkin															
6. Student will tightly roll the napkin around the utensils															
7. Student will place the completed package in the correct bin.															
8. Student will return the bin with the packaged utensils to the correct location															

Table 20: Assessment Rubric: Packaging Utensils

Bibliography

OT Connections. (2009). Retrieved from otconnections.aota.org/more.../aota.../download.aspx

KU Writing Center. (2012, January). Retrieved from KU Writing Center Instructor Writing Resources: http://www.writing.ku.edu/~writing/instructors/guides/documents/Writing_Goals.pdf

Alfaro-LeFevre, R. (2013). *What is Critical Thinking, Clinical Reasoning, and Clinical Judgment?* Retrieved from http://www.elsevieradvantage.com/: http://www.elsevieradvantage.com/samplechapters/9781437727760/9781437727760.pdf

Andrade, H. (2000-2008). *What is a Rubric?* Retrieved from Rubistar: http://rubistar.4teachers.org/index.php?screen=WhatIs

AOTA. (2002). Occupational therapy practice framework: Domain and Process. *American Journal of Occupational Therapy,* 56, 609–639.

Bateman, B. D., & Herr, C. M. (2010). *Writing Measurable IEP Goals and Objectives [Kindle Fire Edition].* (T. Kinney, Ed.) Verona: Attainment Company, Inc. .

Carnegie Mellon. (2012). *Creating and Using Rubrics.* Retrieved January 14, 2013, from Whys and Hows of Assessment: http://www.cmu.edu/teaching/assessment/assesslearning/rubrics.html

Casey, M., Herbst, J., & Stanley, J. (1996). *Red Lace Yellow Lace.* Hauppauge: Barron's Educational Series.

Cawley, E. (2011). *The Student Interview.* Retrieved from Ms. Eleanor's Apples: http://www.mseleanorsapples.com/The-Student-Interview.html

Contributor. (2013). *What does the acroynm RUMBA stand for in nursing terms?* Retrieved from http://wiki.answers.com: http://wiki.answers.com/Q/What_does_the_acroynm_RUMBA_stand_for_in_nursing_terms

Contributors, W. (2012, December 15). *Rubric (academic).* Retrieved from Wikipedia, The Free Encyclopedia.: http://en.wikipedia.org/wiki/Rubric_(academic)

De Paul University. (2001-2012). *Assessment.* Retrieved March 24, 2013, from De Paul Supplemental Teaching Commons: http://condor.depaul.edu/tla/Assessment/TypesRubrics.html

Dodge, N. P. (2007, March 17). *Rubrics for Web Lessons.* Retrieved from Rubrics for Web Lessons: http://webquest.sdsu.edu/rubrics/weblessons.htm

Glor-Scheib, S. J. (2007). Professor of Special Education and Chair of the Education for Exceptional Persons Program in the Special Education and Clinical Services Department of Indiana University of Pennsylvania (IUP). In S. J. Glor-Scheib, *Building Electronic Portfolios* (pp. 15-16). Verona: Attainment Company, Inc.

Hembree, D. (2010, October 19). *How to Write Great Task Analysis*. Retrieved from Voices.Yahoo.com: http://voices.yahoo.com/how-write-great-task-analysis-6999316.html?cat=4

Hemmingsson, H., Egilson, S., Hoffman, O., & Keilhofner, G. (2005). *The School Setting Interview (SSI) Version 3.0*. Retrieved from Model of Human Occupation Theory and Application: http://www.cade.uic.edu/moho/productDetails.aspx?aid=10

Ilott, I. (2004). Challenges and Strategic Solutions for a Research Emergent Profession. *The American Journal of Occupational Therapy, 58*(3), 347-352.

Johnston, T. C. (2010). *Data Without Tears: How to Write Measureable Educational Goals and Collect Meaningful Data* (Kindle Edition ed.). Research Press.

Lowe, N. (2011). Data Literacy for Teachers. *Data Literacy for Teachers*. Port Chester, New York, USA: National Professional Resources, Inc.

Montgomery Schools. (n.d.). Retrieved April 22, 2013, from www.montgomeryschoolsmd.org: www.montgomeryschoolsmd.org

National Center for Research on Evaluation, Standards, and Student Testing (CRESST). (n.d.). *Working Definition of Formative Assessment*. Retrieved April 22, 2013, from Data Use for Improving Learning: http://datause.cse.ucla.edu/fa.php

Pearson Education, Inc. . (2000-2013). *The Advantages of Rubrics*. Retrieved from Teacher Vision: http://www.teachervision.fen.com/teaching-methods-and-management/rubrics/4522.html?detoured=1

Reier, D. (2008, May 22). *NORM-REFERENCED VS. CRITERION-REFERENCED TESTING*. Retrieved from Alta: http://www.altalang.com/beyond-words/2008/05/22/norm-referenced-vs-criterion-referenced-language-tests/

Rogers, J. C. (1983). 1983 Eleanor Clark Slagle Lecture. *American Journal of Occupational Therapy, 37*, 601-616. Retrieved from AOTA.org: http://www.aota.org/Practitioners/Resources/Slagle/1983.aspx

Sackett, D. D. (1996). Evidence-based Medicine - What it is and what it isn't. *BMJ*, 312:71-72.

Swinth, Y., Spencer, K. C., & Jackson, L. L. (2007, June 01). *http://copsse.education.ufl.edu/docs/OT_CP_081307/1/OT_CP_081307.pdf*. Retrieved from COPSSE Center of Personnel Studies in Special Education: http://copsse.education.ufl.edu/docs/OT_CP_081307/1/OT_CP_081307.pdf

The Johnson Center. (2013). *What is a Standardized Test?* Retrieved from The Johnson Center for Child Health and Development: http://www.johnson-center.org/downloads/pdfs/What_is_a_Standardized_Test.pdf

The Minnesota Governor's Council on Developmental Disabilities. (2011, January). *http://www.partnersinpolicymaking.com*. Retrieved from Glossary: http://www.partnersinpolicymaking.com/education/glossary.html

Web Finance, Inc. (2013). *Business Dictionary*. Retrieved from Business Dictionary.com: http://www.businessdictionary.com/definition/accountability.html

Wolf, K., & Stevens, E. (2007). The Role of Rubrics in Advancing and Assessing Student Learning. *The Journal of Effective Teaching , 7*(1), 3-14. Retrieved January 14, 2013, from http://uncw.edu/cte/et/articles/vol7_1/Wolf.pdf

Zelkowitz, A. (2009, April 6). *Using Rubrics to Assess Students with Disabilities' Work*. Retrieved from Teachers Where Teachers Come First: http://blogs.scholastic.com/special_ed/2009/04/using-rubrics-to-assess-students-with-disabilities-work.html

Index